Keep Your
Hopes and
Dreams Alive

Keep Your Hopes and Dreams Alive

Practical advice for a happier life

Michelle Davison Ward

Matador
9 Priory Business Park,
Wistow Road, Kibworth Beauchamp,
Leicestershire. LE8 0RX
Tel: 0116 279 2299
Email: books@troubador.co.uk
Web: www.troubador.co.uk/matador
Twitter: @matadorbooks

ISBN 978 1838592 035

British Library Cataloguing in Publication Data.
A catalogue record for this book is available from the British Library.

Printed and bound by CPI Group (UK) Ltd, Croydon, CR0 4YY
Typeset in 12pt Gill Sans by Troubador Publishing Ltd, Leicester, UK

Matador is an imprint of Troubador Publishing Ltd

DEDICATED TO

"MY FAVOURITE CHILD AND THE OTHER ONE"

Acknowledgements

To my husband and soul mate it has been a bumpy ride but there is no one else I would have at my side.

My mum and dad who truly empowered me to educate myself and others, and to always be kind.

My amazing children who will hopefully one day understand all this philosophical stuff that I harp on about.

My family and friends particularly Suzie, Redders, Lisa Slade and Karen for your ongoing encouragement and support.

To the Friday nighters for my weekly therapy, fun, tears and laughter.

To my guinea pigs Carol, Norman and Karen the first people to do the workshop. I learnt as much from you as you did from me and I will be forever grateful.

My proof-readers; Nayer, Mum, sister Lisa, Suzie, Lisa Redders, Vikki, Hazel, Jess, Sarah Jane, Carol, Glenda and Emma thank you for taking the time to read the drafts, correct my grammar, listen to me going on and on and for your invaluable feedback. You gave me the confidence to continue to the publishing stage.

My amazing and brave clients for sharing their stories and baring their souls. For your openness, honesty and willingness to learn and grow, which continues to inspire me. For allowing me to share your stories to hopefully help others. I have learnt so much from you and will be forever indebted to you.

Finally, to Vikki Maslin such a beautiful soul, thank you so much for the illustrations they are perfect.

I am truly blessed to have you all in my life xx

CONTENTS

INTRODUCTION

This is a SELF-HELP BOOK, if you do not want to help yourself please put the book back!

The book is aimed at people who are lost, lonely, stressed, anxious or depressed and can't see a way forward. The purpose of the book is to give you some thoughts and ideas (tools) on how to help yourself feel better mentally, physically and spiritually, live life with a positive attitude and fulfil your potential.

The information I am sharing with you is what I have gathered is from various books, courses, conversations, TV programmes, research papers, colleagues, friends and family over the years. The book is based on my personal experiences and from my experience of working with people from all walks of life, who have found themselves lost and broken and needing support to change or to get back on track.

It sounds very clichéd, but I realise for a person like me that "doesn't do sympathy" I am really good at helping others, inspiring confidence and self-belief to make changes in their lives.

I want to keep the book simple, so I am not going into too much depth of why people feel depressed, anxious, lost and lonely. I know when I was depressed my brain couldn't take in too much information, concentrating and even thinking was energy sapping, so the chapters aren't too long and are broken up with simple exercises.

For those intellectuals that pick up this book and feel that my English is too basic, please can I ask that you put your ego aside and continue; because you may learn something too.

If you need to make changes in your life but don't know where to start, let me be your inspiration. We need to relight that spark and fan those flames until you are glowing again with hope and purpose.

KEEP YOUR HOPES AND DREAMS ALIVE

CHAPTER ONE
WHAT DO I KNOW?

You might ask, why does this writer think she can help me and what does she know?

Well I know quite a lot actually, I have worked in the "Welfare to Work" sector since 2010, which basically means helping some of the most vulnerable people in society come off benefits and get into work, education or training. I also work with people who have been made redundant and professional people already employed but wanting a change of career.

The reality is that often I am a counsellor, social worker and life coach helping people solve all sorts of real issues in order to move forward in life. During my working life I have successfully helped some of my clients change their lives for the better, having worked with hundreds of clients with a multitude of issues from:

- » Redundancy
- » Homelessness
- » Alcohol and substance misuse
- » Mental health issues
- » Physical disabilities
- » Ex-offenders
- » Anxiety, depression and stress
- » Lack of confidence and self-esteem
- » Bereavement
- » Loneliness and social isolation

In my career I have had jobs where I have to tick boxes for a particular contract, without actually helping a person thoroughly, but this absolutely goes against my morals, virtues and integrity as I want to make a difference to someone's life for the better. I don't want to put a sticking plaster on a gaping wound, when dealing with people's lives it is so much more complex and as I have a conscience, I always want to try to do the right thing.

Sometimes just ticking boxes means setting people up to fail, I could have got someone a job, just to see them lose it soon after because they were not ready to work, and we did not get to the bottom of their REAL issues. I look at the person as a whole, I ask difficult questions to find out what their problems and innermost demons are, I LISTEN carefully to what is said and what is not said and they usually break down and cry (I am good at making people cry.) I realise now that this is a gift and one that I now hold dear, because I feel honoured that people feel safe and secure to bare their soul to me and talk about their darkest fears and emotions. I am an empath, a logical one, that feels others pain but also has a logical approach to problem solving and that is my superpower.

I love the analogy below it shows clearly what sympathy, empathy and apathy mean. If you were sat in your puddle of hopelessness a sympathetic person would sit with you in the puddle, an empath would try to understand your feelings and help you out of the puddle, that is me. Whilst an apathetic person would walk on by and have no sympathy or empathy.

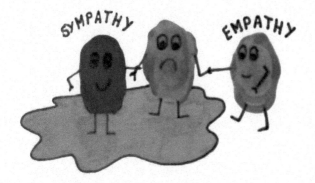

Now on a better note: how do I fix these broken people? Well to be honest, I don't fix people. I can only give them the tools to fix themselves and make the changes needed to recover and become the person they want to be. Essentially the journey is different for everyone. It all depends how broken the person is and where the break is, whether it is physical, mental or their heart/spirit/soul (excuse me for my vagueness with this reference as I am still learning what heart/ spirit/ soul are.) Some people only need to see me once or twice whilst others I can see weekly; for months or a couple of years.

I have written and developed workshops to help people with self-awareness, confidence and self-esteem. I inspire them to act and make changes in their lives, to help themselves be more positive, content and happy.

Life and working with people has taught me that we humans fall into two categories, VICTIMS & SURVIVORS. You may have found yourself in the victim box, feeling sorry for yourself, unable to cope and dwelling about how bad your life is, blaming everyone else for your misfortune. But who is going to change that, well it must be YOU.

You may be a survivor always striving on regardless but due to pressures and events happening in your life you have lost your way and you need a helping hand to guide you in the right direction, so hopefully I can help you too.

At the end of the day no matter what type of person you are, YOU must take responsibility and be willing to make a change in YOUR life. If you keep doing the same things you will always get the same outcomes. There is an old saying, **"You reap what you sow"** So let us start planting some new seeds of hope, after all time does not heal you – YOU HEAL YOU! And time is not on our side.

Hopefully you have found the WILL to make some changes in your life and I can help you take the first steps. This book is filled with examples, activities and ideas to help you move forward. It is something you can return to at any time you feel the need for some guidance and inspiration.

Do something today that your future self will thank you for

So I have told you about my working life but I also want you to know that I was not born with a silver spoon in my mouth and have also suffered on my journey so the next chapter gives you an insight into my life.

CHAPTER TWO
WHO AM I?

I was born 4th October 1972 and was the third child of Ann and Maurice, and 11 months later my younger sister arrived. We lived in a 3 bedroomed house on a council estate; my older brother had his own room, whilst 3 sisters shared a bedroom. Looking back now how my parents coped I have no idea; I think it's just true Yorkshire Grit that kept them going. My mum and dad worked hard to provide for us, but I know what it is to be skint, have ice on the inside of windows and to have to go and ask a neighbour for 50p for the electric meter. Times were hard but no one complained, and my childhood was a happy one, I remember cold snowy winters and long hot summer holidays playing out with friends until dark with none of the menace that faces us nowadays.

My dad was unique, as an ex-Navy man, he could cook, clean, sew, garden, he was very intelligent (you would want him as a friend on Who wants to be a Millionaire) and could fix anything that we broke (which was quite a lot as you can imagine) he was strict and we had to do chores and homework before going out to play. At the time we hated it but looking back now the time and effort he put into us was a precious commodity that I know not everyone is fortunate to receive. He was thoughtful, gentle and kind and he was my superhero.

My mum made our house a home, nurtured us with love and affection, made our clothes, worked 3 jobs when she had to; just to provide for us and she protected us as a lioness would her cubs. Everyone was welcome in our house and with 4 children and all our friends it was often very busy like Kings Cross Station, but it was a house full of love, hopes and dreams.

I was always the sensible one, responsible and mature. I liked order, not chaos. I liked my own company and my siblings used to take the mickey out of me because they thought I was boring. I have always been confident and self-assured although I was quiet and shy (compared to my sisters) I knew my own mind and have always been happy to be my own person and not follow the crowd. I did not get into trouble and I attended school and studied hard, enjoying my education and school.

Even at junior school my teacher Mrs Rigsby saw something in me that I never realised until much later in life.

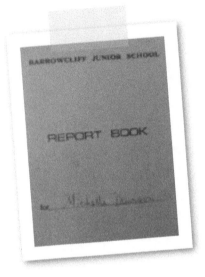

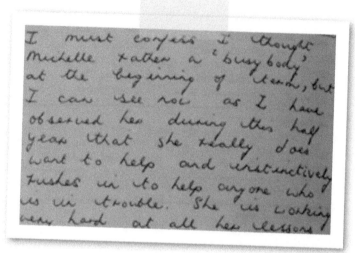

I have always been content positive and optimistic the glass is always refillable and there is always somebody worse off – this has always been my underlying feeling throughout my life and makes me the person I am. I inherited my mum's fat thighs and my dad's varicose veins and a size 16 body, but I have always been comfortable in my own skin. I learnt at a very early age my sisters inherited the skinny DNA both were size 8 and 10 and could eat anything and I mean anything. Size just never bothered me, and I don't know if it was in my DNA not to compare myself to others or it was my upbringing because our parents always showered us with encouragement and confidence no matter our size, capabilities, opinions or behaviour.

I suppose my first experience of sadness and loss was when my grandad died when I was age 10 However, being the logical person that I am it didn't really upset me that much, as my rational thinking is that everyone dies sooner or later. The bigger loss a few months later was that of my beloved dog Benji and I cried for days and days.

Although the family had difficulties with money (that's a whole different story) and not being able to afford the basics sometimes and definitely not luxuries like family holidays, school trips or expensive items, my life continued with the usual problems of teenage years, boyfriends and breakups, making and losing friends, finding alcohol, going out and starting work, leaving school and starting college, dropping out of college, starting another college and generally finding my way in life.

My life took a turn for the worst shortly after my 18th birthday when my aunty age 52 died, followed 2 days later by my new born niece Leoni age just 6 weeks old. My sister was living in our family home and I can still hear the haunting sound of her howling cries when she found her baby had passed away. The carnage of the following weeks was painful as my mum and sister drifted along in a world of grief, my sadness was not for the loss of life but the fact I couldn't do anything to quell the pain for them and it was heart breaking to see them suffering and broken. The only thing I could do to help them was sort out the practical things like; filling out forms, going to the DWP to report the death and organising the funeral. Looking back that is what I am good at, I am the person who says, "don't worry I will sort it" and people know it will get done.

My sister suffered with depression and self-medicated herself for some years, all the while I was there saying "pull yourself together" and "give your head a shake", probably the last thing she needed to hear but me being the responsible, logical person that I am was there pointing out that life still goes on. I thought she was being lazy, I thought that she was playing on the tragedy and I had little sympathy for her. I did not understand her depression at the time, but now having suffered myself I know that trying to get someone to understand depression that has never experienced it, is like trying to explain the colour blue to a blind person who has never seen the colour blue. It is nigh on impossible.

After that period of my life, I met my future husband and saved to buy a house. We bought a lovely cottage near the sea, it had been a holiday home and needed quite a lot of work, but we were up for the task, only the day we signed for the mortgage my partner lost his job. Always looking on the bright side we had a £2,000 cash back mortgage so we could afford the payments for four months whilst he found another job and we would have to wait to do the house up as we wanted.

The next knock was the revelation that my dad had an affair, my dad the person I looked up to, who was not like any other man, the man I idolised. The aftermath was awful, arguments, tears, exhaustion and seeing my mother broken again. They worked through it and my mum stayed with him, but life was never the same again after that.

In 1998 I fell pregnant and was expecting my first child all very exciting until I went for my 20-week scan and was told I had miscarried. Oh well me being me just got on with it, my fall-back position was to think that these things happen for a reason and my logical brain took over, going back to work and getting on with life as always.

I got pregnant again and was anxious throughout my pregnancy hoping everything would be OK, I worked full time up until I was 38 weeks and on the 19th May 2000 I had my son and my life changed forever. He was so chilled out and such a good baby, although I didn't see much of him having returned to work when he was 4 months old (you only got 16 week's maternity leave in those days) I felt guilty for working and not seeing him, but I also felt like I had to work as we needed the money and I wanted him to have all the things I couldn't when I was young.

2003 was another bittersweet year, planning our wedding and looking forward to our hen and stag do's. Only as we were leaving for my hen do my sister got a call to say my brother had been arrested and was looking at a lengthy jail sentence if found guilty. We didn't tell mum until we were coming back from our holiday, as she would have been a complete nervous wreck and had a breakdown instead of a great holiday. We had a fabulous week in Magaluf and would sort out the stress when we got back. So, the wedding arrived, and another trauma came along, my brother-in-law was stabbed on the morning of our wedding and was rushed to hospital, the doctors weren't sure if he would pull through, luckily he did, and the wedding went ahead.

2005 saw the birth of my beautiful daughter and what a different child she was, absolutely into everything, opening child locked Calpol, eating Persil tabs and generally causing chaos. I needed eyes in the back of my head. I still worked full time and juggled being a wife and mother, daughter, sister and friend successfully although feeling spread thinly in all directions, I just about coped. My daughter is unique, she was never a child, she always seemed like an old soul and loved adult company rather than that of other children. She was always mature, intelligent, imaginative and creative. She is a ray of sunshine and continues to be an inspiration to me.

In October 2007 my mother-in-law Joan was diagnosed with lung cancer, during this time we were supported by Margaret and Josie my husband's cousins who came to stay and take care of her. She passed away shortly after in February 2008. I carried on as usual, supporting my husband and family through this difficult period.

Later in 2008 my dad was diagnosed with cancer of the oesophagus, after a massive operation to remove the tumour, whilst having chemotherapy and trying to fight this horrible disease his mother, my nanna died, and he was too poorly to attend the funeral. He passed away shortly after, peacefully on 19 November 2009 and I went back to work a few days later and cracked on with my life. They say things happen in threes and that was the 3 deaths I had dealt with, so I really didn't want any more!

During these years in addition to everyday trials and tribulations, my younger sister lost her way taking drugs and to me existing rather than living but to her "she can't cope with the real world and likes to be in her bubble". Thankfully, my older sister found a way to battle her demons and get her life back on track, she stopped self-medicating, got married and turned her life around. My brother served his prison sentence, stayed with his girlfriend, got married and settled down.

In 2009 whilst working as HR Manager I received an anonymous "poison pen letter" as did the Partners of the firm. I was dealing with my dad's illness and imminent death and felt devastated that someone from work would do this. I requested that we send the letters off to a handwriting specialist, but the outcome was inconclusive and after that the Partners didn't want to do anything further. It sounds pathetic but I loved my job and felt so upset and betrayed that someone could be so nasty and vindictive. It never felt the same after that, I felt like I was being pushed out and didn't know who I could trust and after my father's death I realised life was too short to stay in a place with suspicion and deceit, so it was time for me to move on.

In March 2010 I started working in Welfare to Work and I really enjoyed this new chapter in my life. The job was to help people on disability benefits return to work and some thought that my direct approach would not work. My family call me Nurse Ratchet, as I don't do sympathy, to be fair they are right, however I am very empathetic and find it easy to put myself in someone else's shoes. I worked on a contract with people with disabilities both physical and mental and was helping people change their lives and I loved it, but nothing ever lasts forever, and I was made redundant in 2011.

I inherited some money from my nana, so I decided to take the summer off and spend some time with my children, as one thing the last few years had taught me was that time was precious and my children were growing up quickly.

The final straw was on 19 August 2011 when I found out that my soul mate of 20 years had been having an affair, my world collapsed, my heart broke into a thousand pieces, I physically felt that I had been hit by a truck, my body ached and I couldn't breathe, I couldn't hold a thought in my head, I sobbed so hard for days and days that my head felt like it was going to explode and I slipped into darkness.

My brain was telling me to pull myself together but my heart, spirit, soul or whatever you want to call it was truly broken. Now I knew what my sister and my mum had felt all those years ago and that there was no quick fix for this pain. I functioned on a basic level; my body and brain were working in a fashion, but this new part of me that I was never aware of before, my soul, needed time to heal.

I was so confused by these new feelings that now controlled me, as I had not had to deal with them before, so my logical brain took over and off I went to the library for some books to provide me with an idiot's guide to fixing this debilitating issue. I wanted to know what to do practically to fix myself but there was to be no quick fix, however, the books did help me in some ways.

In November 2011 I found a lump in my breast and had to go and have a biopsy to see if it was cancerous. Luckily it wasn't but I remember not really caring if it had been because I was already feeling so low, I felt death might be the antidote.

I got support from family and friends and I am extremely grateful for that help, but at the end of the day it was up to me to heal myself. I tried a counsellor, but she was too wishy-washy for my personality. So, I put on a brave face to the outside world whilst feeling utterly bereft and devastated on the inside. Being the control freak that I am and the person that can deal with anything life throws at them, I couldn't work out how to get better. One day my sister asked me one of the most important questions of my life "What makes you happy?" I could not answer as I did not know. I had been a daughter, sister, wife, mother and employee and was so busy taking care of everyone else that I had forgotten to concentrate on me. So, sadly at the age of 39, I did not know myself at all and my journey to self-happiness and realisation began. I forgave my husband and my journey with him continues.

In 2014 we received a gift from my lovely friends Karen and Tim to whom I will be eternally grateful. This little ball of fluff that would have a profound effect on me was a puppy and we called him Winston. The joy and unconditional love is immeasurable and he certainly helped my recovery.

In 2015 my brother-in-law had an operation which left him in hospital for 12 weeks and during that time my father-in-law had a stroke being in hospital at the same time as his son for 6 weeks. The stroke had caused irreparable damage and dementia like symptoms, so he had to go into a residential home.

Also, in 2015 my younger sister was diagnosed with breast cancer and had to have an operation, chemo and radiotherapy. She was amazing, taking it all in her stride and getting through the treatment to a happy result that she was given the all clear a year or so later.

My father-in-law passed away suddenly in February 2017, again this was a blessing rather than seeing him suffer in the residential home, not because of the staff, they were brilliant, but his mind slowly deteriorating. As always, I sorted everything out and took care of everyone else. Only this time it was different. I had learnt so much about myself in the last 6 years that my coping strategies were in place and I looked after myself first and foremost. I was aware that this was a very stressful situation on top of an already busy life, and I knew I had to take care of myself; physically, mentally and soulfully and that is what I did to help me cope.

I wrote this book because I know what it is like to be broken to feel utterly bereft and lost. I have some life experience and work experience that can help you with your journey to a more peaceful and contented life. So, let's begin!

CHAPTER THREE
WHO ARE YOU?

In order to move forward and make positive changes in your life you really need to know yourself and what makes you who you are, what makes you happy, sad, anxious, angry, this is called emotional intelligence and then we can explore your hopes and dreams.

You may already be very aware of yourself or you may have no idea, but now it's your turn to think about WHO YOU ARE and write down the pertinent points that made you the person you are today. Think about any instances that broke your heart, mind or body. It could be that you can't pinpoint a traumatic event but instead you have had a series of unfortunate events (as Lemony Snicket would say) so try to make sense of this now. You may have just had a drip drip feed of little things that have built up too. You may have been diagnosed with PTSD, Bi-polar, BPD or other disorders and mental health issues or you may have physical disabilities but that does not have to define you and your future.

So, who are you?

I want you to write down your history, it can be written as a story: a little bit like my opening chapter or a picture of a path or just a list. It can be as little or as many words as you like but you must be honest, if bad things happened to you or you have done bad things now is not the time to shy away from it. These are the things that make us who we are. Just remember this saying which has guided me on my path.

"WHAT HAPPENS TO YOU DOES NOT MATTER, WHAT YOU BECOME THROUGH THOSE EXPERIENCES IS ALL THAT IS SIGNIFICANT, THIS IS THE TRUE MEANING OF LIFE."

Warning – this can be upsetting but it really is worth it to understand yourself better. You may want to do this with someone with you, in a library or café, some where you feel safe. If you have had a traumatic experience and counselling or therapy to accept this, you may want to put an asterix or dot rather that write it down again.

Ok, before you start get a cuppa or glass of water and a box of tissues because this may not be easy. Here are some pointers if you are stuck and don't worry about spelling and grammar, this is just for your eyes only. If you need to stop and have a timeout and come back to this over a period of time, that's fine. Just take your time. Writing things down can be quite daunting as once you put pen to paper it becomes real. However, it can be very liberating too as all those things that you have been fearful of opening up about are released, making your burden lighter to carry.

EXERCISE 1 — KNOW YOURSELF

Think of the following:

- » I was born
- » I lived with my mum/dad/ auntie, grandparents, foster parents, on the street
- » I had sisters and brothers
- » I remember my… birthday because?
- » I went to school, college and remember?

Remember we want a balance so write the good stuff too no matter how small; you will have had some good days!!

- » I remember laughing at
- » I remember smiling at
- » I remember feeling relaxed about

If you don't feel like writing, you can draw a timeline like the example on the following pages:

GOOD	BAD
	1982 grandad and Benji died
1986 Exams	
1989 Exams	
1989 Driving test	
1990 Derek	1990 Aunty Marie & Leoni
1991 Engaged	
1996 New House	1997 Dad affair, mum broken
	1999 miscarriage
2000 Finlay	
2002 New House / Job	
2003 Wedding	2003 Ricky / Jim
2005 Nayer	
	2008 Joan RIP
	2009 Nanna/ Dad RIP
2010 New job	2011 Lost job, relationship and mind
2012 Holiday	
2014 New Job/ Winston	
	2015 Jim hospital/ Jimmy Stroke/ Anj
2016 Promotion	
2017 Training	2017 Jimmy RIP
	2017 Josie RIP

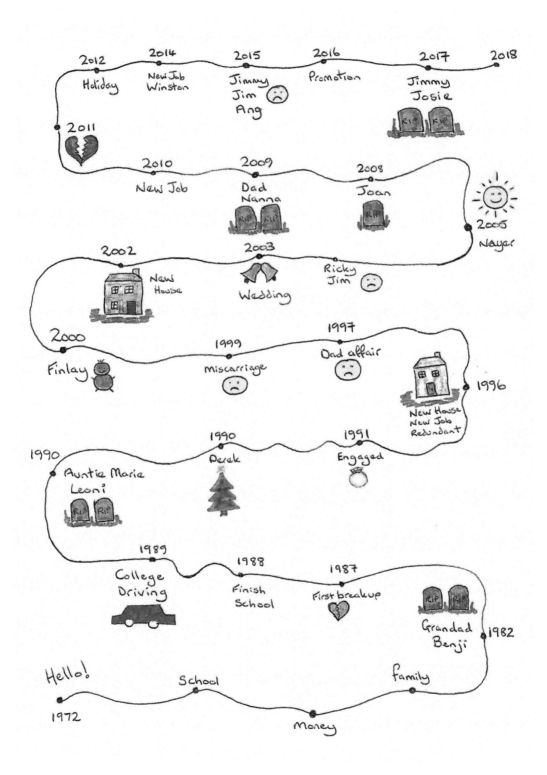

YOUR SPACE TO WRITE!

OK so hopefully you have been brutally honest and have an outline of things that have shaped you. These things are in the past and cannot be changed. It is ok to look back but don't stay there, you need to concentrate on the present and look to the future.

In order to help my clients remember who they are I use a psychology model to personality profile them which everyone finds fascinating and enlightening. The model is based on the work of Carl Jung a renowned psychologist who believed that we are all born with core personality traits, so our personal preferences are already in our DNA and I totally agree. I am one of 4 children to the same parents, brought up in the same house and yet we all have very different personalities. The personality profile is based on the Myers Briggs Indicator and for the work I do it shows what jobs suit certain personality types. I know this is not about getting you a job, but I would still recommend doing this on-line if you can, as it quite insightful and will give you food for thought. It gives you a good starting point if you are feeling lost. It takes approx. 20-30 minutes and asks you a variety of questions. If you" google" search for the 16 preferences test by Carl Jung, you will find it.

YOU have managed to keep going through difficult times in your life and I want you to feel proud of yourself for getting this far.

The reason we are looking at who we are is because it is important to see what has shaped us and there will be some familiar patterns or threads that we can use to help us move forward. We need to be self-aware and emotionally intelligent to know what makes us happy, sad, stressed or depressed and once we can identify these emotions (triggers) we can then learn to manage these feelings.

I do have clients who are very self-aware, they know all of these things already and yet lack the motivation to do anything about their circumstances. And all I can say is; If you keep doing the same things you will get the same outcomes. Perhaps the lack of motivation comes from the lack of courage, because they have a "better the devil you know" attitude. All I know is that we have to be brave and take action.

Quote from a client's workbook:

"Self-awareness for some may bring strong emotions of guilt. This is my main area of negative self-awareness. Depending on what is buried deep within depends on the level of self awareness you allow yourself to discover. Sometimes blame is acceptable if you believe your guilt".

This client's feeling or belief of guilt has made it difficult for her to heal, but with help and therapy she can work through these feelings and help herself to heal.

It is up to YOU to take responsibility for your actions and your life, from this day forward. After all every day is a new day and a gift, a chance to live the life you have always wanted.

CONCLUSION : SELF-AWARENESS IS THE KEY TO HAPPINESS!

CHAPTER FOUR
BURDENS AND INSECURITIES

After reading books and articles on improving confidence and self-esteem it always amazes me that no one wants to talk about the burdens or negative thoughts that we have. Many strategies are to stop thinking about them and put them in a box somewhere in your head, which is fine if you have accepted, confronted and dealt with them but if you haven't then you need to, as these thoughts will continue to eat you up and hold you back.

As part of getting to know yourself you need to recognise the burdens you are carrying around in your head. These burdens are all the negative thoughts and rubbish we keep in our head and as you can imagine this is not good for us; these burdens stop us from moving forward and living life in a positive way.

I want to show you how much these burdens are weighing you down so here's a little exercise.

EXERCISE 2 — VISUALISING BURDENS

Find yourself a large book or chair or object you can hold, and I want you to stand if you can or you can also do this little exercise sitting down.

OK now imagine all of the nasty thoughts, negative stuff and everyday stuff that is stressing you out (BURDENS) and not letting you sleep and pretend it's in a box on the book or chair, now I want you to see how much that weighs.

Hold the chair or book out in front of you with
arms straight…

Keep holding…

Keep holding – KEEP YOUR ARMS STRAIGHT –
NO CHEATING!!!

So is it getting heavier and heavier? YES of course it is,
the longer you hold onto something the heavier it gets!

This is a way to visualise your burdens that are in your head and see them as a weight.
We need to find a way to get that stuff out of YOUR head to lighten the burden.

Easier said than done but you need to try. I am going to give you some ideas but **YOU
HAVE TO TAKE ACTION TO HELP YOURSELF.** It's called self-help for a
reason so if you can't be bothered to help yourself then close the book now.

You're still here, well that is a massive step in the right direction, pat yourself on the
back because YOU are taking control and doing something positive about YOUR life. I
am glad you are here and I really want to help so let's continue.

EXERCISE 3 – MANIPULATING AND VISUALISATION

What are your burdens? They are the deepest darkest thoughts that you can't shake
and the everyday stuff too.

So depending on how bad you're feeling and where you are on your path to recovery
we need a few different exercises. You will need a piece of paper and a pen.

So number one let's start with the really bad stuff. Ok tissues and cuppa at the ready.
I want you to close your eyes and let the thoughts come into your mind. If they come
flooding in take some nice deep breaths and concentrate on one thought at a time,
physically swipe the others away for the moment with your hand. You can only focus
on one thing at a time.

So now we know one of the issues, there are a few ways to deal with this information. I want you to write it down, just a few words of the thing in your mind.

Now we know what is bothering you we can look at releasing it!

EXERCISE 4 — RELEASE THE BURDENS

1. Write it down and tear it up!

Write down the issue and tear the paper up and put it in a bin and say out loud I am not going to think about *that* anymore.

2. Write on a stone and throw it in a river, lake or the sea.

3. Use the F**k it bucket

A few of my clients use the "F**k it bucket" method. Where by they think of the issues and raise their hand to their head and imagine pulling the thought out and put it in the metaphorical "F**k it bucket," as it is a waste of time worrying about something they cannot control.

4. Use the "Damn it doll" made and sold by the lovely ladies from the church.

When your day has started wrong and things go from bad to worse here's a little DAMMIT DOLL to help you lift the curse, take it gently by the leg and find some place to slam it, then as you knock the stuffing out, shout
DAMMIT! DAMMIT! DAMMIT!

5. Hands together and throw away

You can also close your hands together and speak into your closed hands then throw your hands open to release the issue into the air.

6. Write it down and do something about it

I find writing my issue on a piece of paper and then turning the paper over and writing 3 positive things I am going to do about it helps me deal with the issue.

Example: On the front of the paper I write something that is bothering me;

> My relationship
> with my husband

On the back I write

> 1. Talk more – make the effort
>   to communicate better
>
> 2. Date nights once a month
>
> 3. Bury in garden (only joking)

Be specific and make sure you do the actions you have written on the back. Put some dates or deadlines if action is needed and make sure they are realistic or this is pointless!

Some things we just cannot change, we simply cannot undo what has happened in the past, we can't stop someone from dying, we can't un-see the horrors we have seen or committed, we can't stop people leaving our lives, we can't stop ageing or becoming ill, we can't stop children growing up and leaving home, we can't stop losing our jobs or homes.

BUT WE CAN CHANGE THE WAY WE THINK ABOUT THOSE THINGS.

I write on the front of the paper   and on the back I write

I miss my dad
(he is dead by the way)

1. Remember the fun times

2. He is still alive in me and my children

3. He would not want me to be sad

7. Talking to someone

Talking is one of the best ways of releasing your burdens. If you can talk to friends or family, I would highly recommend it, however, sometimes we find it easier to talk to complete strangers. Depending how low you are feeling you may want to speak to your GP about counselling. There are also many organisations and charities that can help people, you can find a list at the back of this book.

Some Hospices also offer bereavement counselling so give them a call or get someone to ring and enquire for you. Sometimes you can self-refer without going through a doctor. There are many organisations and charities that help with alcohol and substance abuse, but YOU yes YOU have to take the first step to helping yourself. If you can't go alone please, please, please ask someone to go with you.

I know personally I had always struggled with talking about my emotions and bottled things up, I am a very private person and don't like people knowing my business. I struggle to talk to others about my feelings, so for me personally I do find writing stuff down really helpful. Believe me I have changed, and I am a total advocate for talking and expressing yourself, to the point I have written a book about it. Who would have thought that would ever happen? Well I am making the most of my lessons in life and I am the most content I have ever been.

Please start working on these different exercises, try different methods and see what works for you.

One of my clients couldn't see the point in doing this as her problems would still be there and she felt that there was nothing she could do about any of her issues. She was in a very negative mindset and was not open to the exercises that I suggested. I went away and considered how I could get my point across. At our next meeting I used the following analogy.

Imagine you have been shopping and you are carrying several bags of heavy shopping – you do not want to get rid of any of the shopping, but they are weighing you down. The purpose of the exercise is to stop and rest, release the burden if you can or after you have rested pick it up and carry on.

So, depending how bad I feel I do Exercise 4 once a week or once a month, if you are really low I would suggest these exercises daily or weekly, with a cuppa and box of tissues.

Once we are aware of stresses and issues, we can start to release them, it is a positive action and the burden on our minds become lighter, helping us to move forward. So, keep visualising and releasing the burdens.

EXERCISE 5 — MIND MAP

The other exercise I often use and recommend is something called a Mind Map or Brain Dump. Sometimes my brain goes into overdrive and it feels like it is going to explode. I find it hard to hold a clear thought in my mind, so this helps me categorise the issues that are bothering me.

This exercise is to write down everything that is in your brain and I mean everything. I draw a flower and each petal is a different area of my life. My Mind map is like this because I like structure and order but yours can be any shape size, messy or tidy. Just write down what comes into your mind. This can be anything from shopping and jobs to do to ambitions, goals and fears. Again, depending how full your brain is or how stressed you feel, do this daily, weekly or monthly.

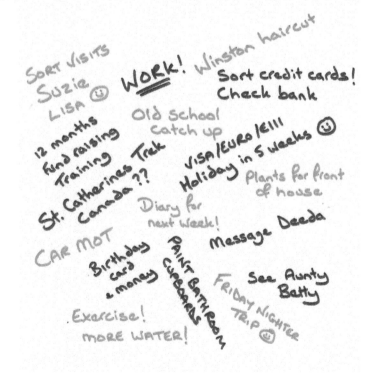

SPACE IN BOOK FOR READER TO WRITE...

You don't need to do anything with this picture it's just a release. If you feel that you do need to do something with this information, then you may want to write a "jobs to do list" to start working through some of the issues that have come out. Please be careful with lists as they can be quite overwhelming, if you put too many things on the list and too much pressure on yourself you may feel like a failure if you do not get through the list as quickly as you would want to.

You may actually need to write a few lists and give yourself sensible amounts of time to get things done. See chapter 15 on goal setting for more help with this.

CONCLUSION:

IDENTIFY YOUR BURDENS AND FIND A WAY TO RELEASE THEM!

YOU NEED TO LIGHTEN YOUR LOAD — LET IT GO!

CHAPTER FIVE

LOSS AND SADNESS

Whilst we are getting everything out in the open, part of your burdens and reason for stress, anxiety and depression could be because of the loss of something.

Loss can be the loss of anything, a person or animal dying, the loss of your health, the loss of your youth, the loss of your hair, your job, your children growing up, or the future you had planned.

I have worked with many clients that have lost their jobs, childhood, health and loved ones and they have never come to terms with that loss. We need to take time to grieve these losses and remember IT IS OK TO BE SAD. For some clients I recommend that they sit down once in a while and think about their loss, listen to sad music or watch a sad film, have a duvet day and allow yourself to feel sad and cry, it is a release and sometimes good for you. (Obviously doing it every day is not.) Remember you may need professional help to deal with these emotions so speak to your GP, hospice, Relate, and other organisations for professional advice.

I remember watching a Billy Connolly documentary about death and someone saying grief is something that you cannot go around, over or under you must go through it and so you must face your demons and come to terms with your loss. In order to move forward we need to ACCEPT and come to terms with what has happened.

A friend of mine was grieving for the loss of her son and she felt she could never listen to the song played at his funeral, whilst having counselling the counsellor asked her why she couldn't listen to the song and my friend said she felt like she would break. Eventually she did listen to the song and she did cry and cry but afterwards she felt better for it. Sometimes the fear of something is much worse in our heads than the reality. So, it is learning to overcome the fear and letting go. Of course, even now she has difficulty hearing the song as it evokes so many sad memories, but sometimes instead of avoiding we need to face our fears, let the sadness wash over us and be in the moment with it.

I remember a client coming to see me about getting a job however, she was suffering from depression and anxiety and after talking she admitted that she had never dealt with the loss of her husband, she had pushed herself into work and keeping busy so as not to face the truth. Eventually 2 years on the work and burdens got too much and she had to finish work. I suggested that she should go and see her GP and she said she had already, she explained how she felt and the response from the GP was "It has been 2 years you should be over it by now". She felt stupid and pathetic and she wanted to "pull herself together" (her words) but she couldn't. I was so angry that she had plucked up the courage to say something to her GP only to be met by such a disparaging response. The lady did complain to her normal GP and was referred for bereavement counselling, so please don't give up at the first hurdle.

Grief is a personal journey but it is one you must take so YOU need to find a way of coping with it whether that is talking about it, writing about it, screaming, singing, drawing, painting, seeking counselling and professional help but whatever it takes you must go through it. We are all different and our journey through grief is also different and so therefore it will take as long as it takes.

Remember it is ok to feel sad. This is a perfectly normal human emotion and it is ok to cry, so please be kind to yourself and give yourself time to grieve, whether it's a person, pet, job, health or the future you had planned. Give yourself time to ACCEPT the loss and come to terms with it. Be mindful of anniversaries, birthdays, Christmas and family gatherings as all can cause overwhelming emotions and be a trigger for anxiety and depression. Think about what you may do on these days and be honest with your emotions and how you feel. When we put on a brave face, bottle things up and tell everyone we are OK when we do not feel OK, our brains get confused with the mixed signals. Remember it is OK to be sad.

We must allow ourselves time to heal and be kind to ourselves, do not put too much pressure on yourself to be better in weeks or months. I had always gone through life with my mind and body functioning well and thought that I was a healthy and whole person. It was not until my heart was broken that I realised we are made up of 3 parts. When I was broken my body and brain worked in a fashion but there was a huge hole and feeling of utter loss and emptiness that I couldn't function properly. My sister explained that this was my heart (spirit or soul) and to a logical person this was an epiphany.

It took me some time to realise in order to heal I must take care of my Mind, Body and Soul as all three are implicitly linked to our well-being. However, having never really being in touch with my heart/spirit/ soul I struggled to know what I needed to do. I saw a quote that is totally appropriate for me as my mind is constantly busy, looking for answers, trying to fix everything and control external forces (which you can't by the way). My next step is to try meditation to quiet my mind. The point is being open minded as to what can help you heal and trying these things until you find what works for you.

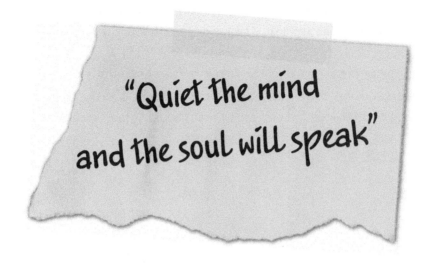

"Quiet the mind and the soul will speak"

Imagine you are a three legged stool with the three legs representing your Mind, Body and Soul and if one or more of the legs are broken you will fall.

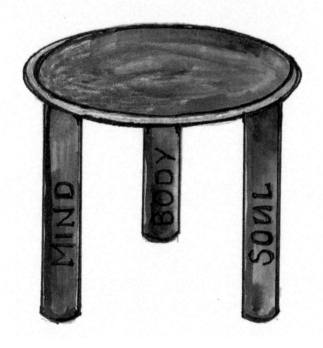

Quite a few of my clients have asked me where to start if all three legs are broken, well the answer is the body because if we do not look after that the other two parts won't work either. One of my clients described herself as a frisbee as all three legs to her stool are broken, she has been under the mental health team for many years and has various mental health conditions including BPD and disassociation disorder. I suggested that we looked at her lifestyle and eating to help fix her mind, so I asked her what she ate, to which she asked Why? She said no-one in the mental health teams had ever asked her what she ate. When she finally confessed to what she ate it was very little as she had suffered from anorexia from a young age and she did not have a good relationship with food. She basically lives on white coffee with sugar and blue WKD. Well I am no doctor, but my guess is that a brain can work effectively with such little nutrients.

I have read various books and articles on brain function and I know we need to feed it, for it to work properly. One of the things we need is something called dopamine (I am not going into scientific specifics) but part of its work affects our moods. Things that reduce our dopamine levels are sugar, caffeine and alcohol which was essentially my client's diet, so my thoughts were that we needed to change her diet to help her mind. Our aim was to replace coffee with decaf coffee and to replace the WKD with smoothies or soup. So please just think about what you eat and feed your body and start with some small changes to feed your mind and soul.

I want you to imagine your body with a power station as a brain and a control room in your stomach and your spirit living in your heart.

Now image the control room checking the nutrients in what you eat and making decisions to send these limited nutrients to the critical areas of your body first; heart, lungs, liver etc. Your brain, the power station is only lit by a tiny pilot light because you never eat enough fuel to power up the whole power station, and whilst you are starving your brain you never have any energy to do anything to help your soul/spirit either so that the spark in there goes out completely.

We can make really small changes that have a large impact on our wellbeing, so start small with the very basics. Am I eating the right things, drinking enough water, getting enough sleep, getting enough exercise and taking the correct medication and getting the right therapy? Remember therapy can be talking, meditation, walking, earthing, bubble baths, hobbies and interests. If not, that is where you start, please get help and advice from your doctor or practice nurse if need be. I use my hand and 5 fingers as a reminder everyday to look after myself and I ask my clients to do the same.

Often clients come back and say they are not well, and I hold my hand up and say are you doing the 5 basics?

1. Eating well (plenty of fruit and veg – no caffeine, sugar, alcohol, processed foods)

2. Drinking enough water (at least 2 litres a day)

3. Exercising (at least 30 minutes a day)

4. Sleeping (6-8 hours)

5. Taking meds and/or therapy (therapy can be art, talking, walking, meditation etc)

Below is a list of things which I feel help my mind, body and soul but this is a work in progress and yours may vary. Please take time to think about each area and add to the lists to help yourself heal and move forward.

MIND	BODY	SOUL
Healthy Food	Healthy Food	Healthy Food
Water	Water	Water
Sleep	Sleep	Sleep
Exercise	Exercise	Exercise
Meds	Meds	Meds
Forgiveness		Forgiveness
Reading		Candles
Hobbies		Crystals
Puzzles		Meditation
Yoga	Yoga	Yoga
Pilates	Pilates	Pilates
Travel	Travel	Travel
Relaxation	Relaxation	Relaxation
Bubble bath	Bubble baths	Bubble baths
Social Interaction		Helping others
Work		Nature
Art and creativity		Art and creativity
Writing		Writing

Please be mindful of which part of you is broken, my heart break caused my depression and although drugs may have helped, I chose to avoid this course of action, instead I concentrated on fixing my heart. I feel like joy and love is the glue that we need to fix a broken heart, it sounds so clichéd, but I know it is true for me. It is about investing time in yourself to understand the basic things that make you feel better, the simple things in life and going back to basics; walking in the woods, paddling in the sea, reading a book, exercise, listening to music. On that note (did you see what I did there) music is a very powerful mood changer, so check your play list and see what you are listening to. Sometimes instead of listening to sad songs we need something upbeat. Again, be aware of what changes your mood and do more of the good stuff.

I healed my heart, I now imagine that it is made of thin red glass that has been glued back together, the cracks are still there but the joy I feel from helping others is helping to cover those cracks making it stronger. It is still a very fragile thing, but I keep it open to love and joy and all the good things in life to help it heal. I know some build a wall around themselves after their heart has been broken and do not feel they can trust anyone again and I imagine them like the Grinch, their heart shrinking not able to love or feel love. Well I would say believe in yourself and your power to heal and believe in others, there are some good people out there, be open to love and joy and your heart will repair.

There are some practical things you can do to help you with loss.

1. Let it all out, do not bottle up your emotions, if you feel angry, sad, frustrated, lonely, bereft this is all perfectly normal so let it out – be honest with others how you feel. If you don't know say "I don't know"

2. Be kind to yourself – It is ok to feel sad

3. Get some exercise – it releases endorphins in our brain and helps us feel better

4. Look after yourself, drink plenty of water and eat fresh food

5. Try to keep a routine (go to bed at the same time and get up at the same time)

6. Get some sleep (we need approx. 7.5 hours per night)

7. Avoid self-medicating with drugs and alcohol

8. Speak to someone – GP, counsellor, Samaritans, family or friends

9. Write a journal or just write as a way of getting things out of your head

10. Laugh and laugh some more. It sounds weird at a time of grieving, but laughter is the best medicine

HEALING takes **TIME**, but time alone cannot fix us. We must also have the **INTENTION** to heal ourselves. I remember talking to my husband and telling him that I had forgiven him for what he had done to me. He on the other hand could not forgive himself, he said he couldn't and because at the time he had no intention to forgive himself then there was no way he could possibly heal, and his own guilt was poisoning him and stopping him from moving forward.

The reason I forgave was not for him but for me. I did not want to poison myself with feelings of bitterness and anger as I knew this would destroy me. For me it was a logical question, why would I hurt myself and not forgive? I know emotional people may find this harder to do but in order to heal yourself you must **forgive others**. This is not going to be easy for people that have been emotionally or sexually abused, betrayed or suffered trauma and this will take professional help and therapy but it can be done. I cannot even begin to comprehend how someone who has been through such times will heal, but I know it is possible and I take inspiration from other survivors such as Maya Angelou, Oprah Winfrey, Katie Piper, Axl Rose (Guns and Roses) Emimen and many more. You will be surprised if you google this.

> "Not forgiving someone is like drinking poison and expecting the other person to die – unknown"

I have spoken to many people who are suffering from guilt from the loss of something; asking what if? Why? If only I had done something differently. I have done this myself and it is a total waste of time and energy, the truth is it does not stop the thing from happening therefore we must accept it and **forgive ourselves**, only with the intention to heal will you heal.

A client of mine had been suffering with depression and anxiety on and off for a period of 10 years and in our workshops, she shared with us that she felt guilty about the death of her son as he had died in her care. We discussed the concept of forgiveness and she understood that was something she had to do to heal but she felt she could not forgive herself and felt that she didn't deserve to be happy. We discussed bereavement counselling to talk openly about her guilt and fears and this was the next step for her to take on her path to recovery.

> "You will begin to HEAL when you let go of past hurts, forgive those who have wronged you and learn to forgive yourself for your mistakes. - unknown"

Finally, it is no good just taking time and having the intention to heal, we must also take **ACTION.** I am so pleased that you have picked up this book as it means you have the intention and are hopefully willing to take action to heal yourself. Action means loving yourself, doing the things it takes to heal yourself. Being kind to yourself, eating properly, exercising, taking time for yourself without feeling guilty. I know it is difficult, but self-care is the starting point of your recovery.

CONCLUSION: HEALING = TIME + INTENTION + ACTION

CHAPTER SIX

DEPRESSION AND DESPAIR

There is a difference between feeling sad and depressed. Sadness is a normal emotion it is not an illness or disease. Unfortunately, the media shows us that we should be happy all of the time, but that is fake and unrealistic. So, when we are sad, we think it is wrong to feel this way, part of this is due to our culture in the UK to be strong and have a "stiff upper lip". Also being told not to cry from a young age, "be brave" or "I will give you something to cry for" has prevented us from showing our true feelings. But it is fine, and we are allowed to feel sad, if we bottle up these emotions it is like a bottle of pop building pressure waiting to explode or a dam waiting to break, this may result in mental health issues.

Depression on the other hand has been said to be a chemical imbalance in the brain and we may need medication for this. However, there is other research out there to suggest that depression maybe an inflammation in the brain caused by what we eat, drink, medications we take and the environments we live in. Speak to your GP before you self-diagnose, however, I do think the quote below is just as apt, in some pictures it states it comes from Sigmund Freud and others William Gibson, either way I like it!

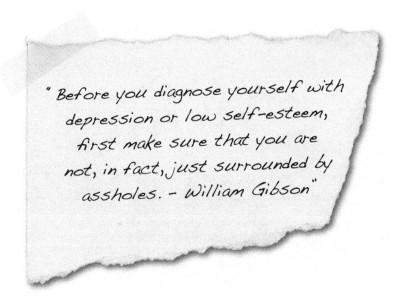

" Before you diagnose yourself with depression or low self-esteem, first make sure that you are not, in fact, just surrounded by assholes. - William Gibson"

Be aware that medication can only go so far to help with a chemical imbalance in the brain and that it will not fix a broken heart/soul/spirit, and maybe that's where your problem really lies! Do not stop taking your medication but be aware that there are little things you can do to help yourself too.

I will try to explain what depression means to me from a known counselling model.

As we go through life imagine that we constantly walk over a pit with a layer of ice over it. If we have no burdens and stress weighing us down, we constantly walk over the ice and it will never break, and we lead a contented life.

Once we add the weight of many stresses we carry and burdens to our load the ice becomes thinner with each crossing and amount of weight and eventually the ice will break. We end up in a pit of despair and for all of us the amount of time we remain there differs.

For me personally this felt like it was pitch black, I was always freezing cold, treading water in an open endless sea and I was so physically and mentally drained and exhausted I could hardly keep my head above the water. Although I wasn't suicidal, I did not care if I slipped under the water and never woke up because I was so tired. I was depressed, I felt no emotions, no sadness, joy or anger I was completely void of emotion. I struggled to take information in my brain, and it was difficult to take in what people were saying to me. I felt like I was in another world, in thick fog or the other side of glass and communication was very trying. Just getting up and dressed took an immense amount of energy and some days I couldn't find that energy and stayed in bed.

All of my clients with depression describe it as darkness, fog, or being in a bubble feeling isolated from the real world. One client described her depression as standing in the dark on the edge of a cliff waiting to fall over and she was hoping for a gust of wind to blow her over the edge to end the pain and suffering.

There was no light bulb moment and I cannot pin point when or how I found the energy (I like to think I always had the will) to try and get out of the pit, maybe months after the physical pain had become less, I think my body did go into self-preservation mode whereby all I needed to do was the basics; breathe, eat and sleep. Although as with most depression sufferers a good night's sleep does nothing for our exhaustion levels. What I do know is it takes every ounce of energy and WILL to drag yourself out, but it can be done with lots of self-care. With your own will and the help and support from others you can climb out of the pit and continue on your journey. It can take a while so please be patient and kind to yourself.

Sadly, once our mind and/or soul has been broken, just like we break a bone in our body, there will always be a scar and a weakness. We can never go back to the person that we were, this again is a loss and I really struggled with this for some time as I wanted to be the happy and confident old me, why should I be different because of someone else's doing? My logical brain took over and I finally accepted the losses and decided I had to move on vowing to learn from these losses. I know I am a better person than I was before, I am now whole: understanding the 3 parts of me that I need to nurture. I can honestly say if I was to live my life over again I would do it exactly the same way. (Only I would have bought more colours of those shoes in Milan and a terrace of houses in Teeside for £2k — my only regrets) I now accept all loss as learning or enlightenment as there is always something new to learn. There is always the worry that we may fall back into the pit should another trauma affect us and I think with depression it will always be there and be a part of you. I remember watching a documentary about mental health and the sufferer saying his depression was like a letter in the post waiting to drop through the letter box. That is true for all of us but there are ways to minimise the risk of this happening to us. I know my heart will be broken again because that is life, but now I know how to deal with it, I will be kind to myself and patient and follow my own advice in this book!

I know my sister won't mind me sharing this but in order to help her depression she has a good routine and tries to keep herself busy to keep the black beast at bay. She exercises regularly, eats healthily, works, and has a timetable of hobbies and interests to keep her occupied. There are some days and weeks when it creeps back in and being self-aware she realises this, as do I and now we ride the wave instead of sinking. Keeping your life balanced is what it's all about.

I also had a client who was a very positive person and was grateful for her life and all she had however she suffered with clinical depression. She took her medication and carried on a good routine of getting up, dressed and going out helping in a charity shop and doing a part time paid job but she felt numb. She did not feel joy, sadness, anger or any other emotion. Her psychiatrist had advised that she keep doing what she was doing and eventually she would start to "feel" again. This is something she continues to work on.

EXERCISE 6 – VISUALISE YOUR BALANCE AND ENERGY LEVELS

THE SEESAW

Imagine your life as a seesaw and you are in the middle, bad things happening on one side and good on the other. When the bad/ negative and stressful things start to weigh us down we must do twice as much of the good stuff to keep ourselves balanced so we do not tip and slide downwards into the pit of despair again.

Sometimes we don't feel like doing any good things because we are so drained and have no energy, so it is really important to keep our energy levels up in order to do the good stuff that makes us feel better! The key to balance is self-awareness, knowing what is good and bad for you. People often list lots of bad stuff, but you also need to know what makes you feel good too. We will explore this later in the book.

THE BATTERY

You need to be self-aware of your own feelings, taking time out to understand how you feel is really important. You also need to be aware of external pressures and people wanting a piece of you and your time. Imagine you are a battery and every time you do something for a person (especially someone who doesn't appreciate it) it drains your battery; every bit of stress and negative situations drain your battery. So, you need to STOP doing things that drain you, remove negative people and situations from your life and do more positive things.

Please allow yourself some YOU time to concentrate on your own wellness. I remember being completely rubbish at giving myself time to heal to begin with as I always felt guilty for doing "nothing" but after going through a difficult period of my life with physical illness (from stress) my osteopath said some very magical and life changing words to me. "I give you permission to do nothing because you need to get well". So, I will pass on the same message to you. "I GIVE YOU PERMISSION TO DO NOTHING BECAUSE YOU NEED TO GET WELL" If you do not give yourself time to rest and heal then please realise that your recovery time will take much longer.

No doubt you would give this advice to others if/when they are struggling with life, so you actually need to listen to your own advice and be kind to yourself and start to invest time in yourself and your wellbeing.

CONCLUSION:

YOU ARE THE MASTER OF YOUR SEESAW (LIFE) — TRY TO KEEP IT BALANCED!

YOU ARE IN CHARGE OF YOUR BATTERY — KEEP IT FULL!

CHAPTER SEVEN

ANXIETY AND OVERTHINKING

I have always struggled with the concept of people suffering with anxiety and depression, because for me my depression meant feeling nothing, I was void of all emotions so how can people be depressed and anxious at the same time? I realise now that depression is different for each of us and after talking to clients, I think maybe the depression comes after the anxiety and panic when we feel exhausted and fall into the pit of despair. This can happen daily, weekly, monthly etc. and this will be different for every one of us.

One of my clients explained his anxiety really clearly for me to understand. He said imagine a gauge with a needle pointing to the left calm section and with each bit of stress and pressure the needle moving quickly to the right danger zone, then it just uncontrollably flicking rapidly across the gauge. At this point he went into a panic, couldn't breathe and could not focus his thoughts or rationalise anything.

The way he dealt with this was to concentrate on his breathing and slowly calming down to a point where he could think straight. There are different coping strategies to use to deal with anxiety and panic attacks and it would be worth speaking to your GP regarding this. Exercise, focusing on a task, meditation, music, breathing exercises and yoga are all known to have benefits to help combat anxiety.

"The greatest weapon against stress is our ability to choose one thought over another – William James"

One of my client's anxiety was overthinking and analysing everything, questioning things repeatedly in her mind to the point she felt her head was going to explode. It's like having a thousand search tabs open on a computer at once all running with various bits of data. She said even going out with friends which she really enjoyed would put her in a state of anxiety, worry and panic to the point that sometimes she didn't make it out and then she felt a whole raft of other emotions like guilt and being ashamed, hating that she could not control the anxiety. Then it becomes a vicious cycle that we need to try and stop.

"THINK TOO MUCH AND YOU WILL CREATE A PROBLEM THAT WAS NOT THERE IN THE FIRST PLACE – UNKNOWN"

I don't feel that I suffer from anxiety although maybe I still do not know myself well enough to know the signs. I can totally relate to my brain feeling like it's going to explode because of too many thoughts, but I think that's from a busy work / life situation. On the other hand, because I do not feel stress knowingly in my brain, my body has another way of telling me I am stressed and that I need to calm down. I suffered from migraines for years which turned into black outs and fainting episodes as well as dizziness to the point that I couldn't get out of bed. I was diagnosed with migraine affected vertigo, essentially, I do not get the severe headaches that I used to get with migraine now I get vertigo instead. The reason for these episodes? Well that would be stress! The specialists told me I had to change to prevent these episodes, so guess what? I took their advice and changed. I cut out caffeine which was difficult because I had 8 cups of tea a day, but I did it because it would help me, I drank more water and got more exercise and took time out to calm down and release the stress. So now I try to listen to my body, and I know that prevention is the best medicine, I have a Secret Recipe for being Calm which helps me with my stress levels, which I will share with you later in the book.

> " I will breathe. I will think of solutions.
> I will not let my worry control me. I will not let
> my stress level break me. I will simply breathe
> and I will be okay because I don't quit
> – Shayne McClendon "

If you have been advised by your GP, counsellor, medical professional or family or friends to change and to do something to help yourself then YOU NEED to do it. When I had a bad back the physio told me to do exercises every morning and to start Pilates to help with my back pain, guess what I took his advice, and did it and my back is better. It is not rocket science!

If I relate my stress and pain to anxiety and panic attacks, I would also say prevention is the best medicine too. After talking through what makes us anxious it seems very similar to what makes us stressed so it is knowing the triggers and trying to prevent them when and where possible.

There is an analogy about a bucket of sand. Every day we wake up with an empty bucket and every stressful thing that happens to us throughout the day adds a spadeful of sand into the bucket. For example;

» The alarm goes off late
» You can't find one of your shoes
» You are late for an appointment or work
» The bus is running late
» A bill or demand comes in the post
» You burn the toast
» The children are not ready
» Etc.

Each action puts more sand into the bucket until it overflows and you have a meltdown and can't take no more. This can take days, weeks, months but at some point, it will overflow. So, prevention is the best way to stop our buckets overflowing.

I know we can't prevent some things happening, but we can take action about the small things to help us deal with the big things. For example, being late for school or work;

- » Ensure the alarm is set properly
- » Prepare our clothes the night before
- » Prepare pack lunches / food the day before
- » Leave the house on time

One of my clients suffered so much from anxiety that it led to self-harm, her explanation was that she felt so anxious inside that she felt self-harming gave her the release she needed from all the tension. She said she physically felt the bad stuff leaving her body with the blood from the wound and then she felt relief, this was quickly followed by a raft of other emotions once she felt aware of what she had done. She was scared at the amount of blood, guilty for what she had done, ashamed, physically in pain, the list goes on. She is working with a counsellor to help with the self-harm. If this is something that you are experiencing speak to your GP/ Mental Health team.

I also had a client that had an eating disorder, she was not anorexic, and it was not about what she saw in the mirror, but she chose not to eat as this was the only control she felt she had in her life when all external factors were out of her control.

My belief after speaking to others and using my own experience is that these emotions and actions come from our lack of ability to express ourselves and/or control what is going on around us. We bottle up our emotions and feelings to the point where we; are anxious, have panic attacks, collapse, stop eating, self-harm, self-medicate, lock ourselves away or whatever mechanism we use (which are not helpful) to try to gain some sort of control back but it doesn't actually work. What we should be doing is expressing our emotions and feelings, getting the stuff out of our heads and preventing ourselves getting to breaking point in the first place.

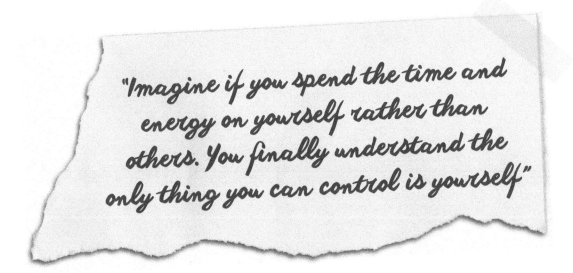

"Imagine if you spend the time and energy on yourself rather than others. You finally understand the only thing you can control is yourself"

One of my clients on my courses has made huge improvements from cutting out energy drinks and caffeine (5-6 cans a day) so she is sleeping better. She also cries a lot now which is great as she was always told not to cry and bottling things up IS NOT GOOD FOR US. She is also very honest about how she feels so her head and heart are not in conflict anymore. She is open when people ask how she is and instead of saying fine (which stands for Freaked out, Insecure, Neurotic and Emotional) she says I am not good or not doing very well etc. It might be uncomfortable for the person asking the question but now she feels so much better just for being honest. Her mind and emotions are saying the same thing instead of conflicting information.

I believe resentment and anger are also triggers for our mental health issues, looking back over my life I have been very resentful and angry about other people but have not been aware that this is what I was feeling. Now I am more in touch with my feelings I can understand them and talk about them. For example; when I was younger, I felt resentment towards my sisters as they were always out partying whilst I was at home studying and acting like a grown up whilst they were being irresponsible and selfish. This was not their fault this was about my expectations of people and how they should act. Looking back, I made my choices and they made theirs. What I needed to do was accept we were different.

Likewise, I would resent my husband for going out whilst I was looking after the kids and I felt he was selfish putting his friends before me and the children. I know many people feel resentment about family, friends, children, employers, colleagues etc. and if we don't deal with this emotion then it starts to eat us up to the point that we can't talk to the other person leading to feelings of hatred.

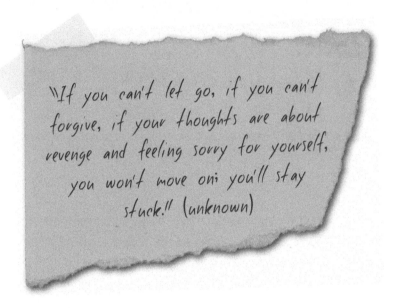

"If you can't let go, if you can't forgive, if your thoughts are about revenge and feeling sorry for yourself, you won't move on; you'll stay stuck." (unknown)

I would say the best way to deal with these emotions is to talk to the person and explain how and why they make you feel like they do. I did this with my husband, and he took on board what I said. In work situations I have also spoken out and sometimes employers have not cared about my feelings or opinions, in which case I removed myself from the situation causing me stress, life is too short to work in an environment that is not good for you. I know a lot of people that will live with the status quo because they do not like conflict and speaking to someone about how they feel may lead to an emotionally charged argument. I say be brave, pick your time wisely, when both have at least been fed, watered and are not tired. Sometimes timing is everything.

One way or the other once you let people know how they make you feel you will get your answer. It might not be the one that you wanted but at least you will know, and you can take steps to change the situation. If not, things will stay the same or deteriorate further. I say be BRAVE talk about how you feel. If someone does not care enough to listen, maybe this person is not the right one for you.

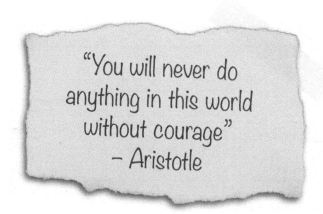

"You will never do anything in this world without courage"
– Aristotle

So, it's back to triggers, knowing exactly what triggers our anxiety and depression and preventing where we can and learning better coping strategies where we cannot control external forces.

Once we understand the triggers, we can take steps to help us with everyday activities and lead a better life with peace of mind. We need to take time to understand them and minimise them.

EXERCISE 7 — KNOW YOUR TRIGGERS

OK you should be used to this by now, get a cuppa and a box of tissues because it's time for you to think about what triggers your anxiety, depression and negativity. Take your time and really think about this carefully, because once you know what the triggers are you can start to work on them. Try to be specific so don't just put "work" say what it is about work or "family" say who or what makes you feel bad.

Some clients really struggle when I ask them to think or write things down. They feel overwhelmed and overthink things. I am not asking you to find the cure for cancer! So think small, if we start with the small stuff the rest will follow.

What little things called triggers are causing you suffering, stress, depression, and anxiety? You need to be very honest and remember the issue may lie with you and not with others.

Here is a list of titles which may help with yours:

Tiredness	Betrayal
Hunger	Bereavement
Hormones / menstrual cycle	Validation
Money	Decision making
Work	Abuse
Family	Loneliness
Friends	House/ home environment
Health	Children
Caring about others opinions	Not letting people down
Trust issues	High expectations
Moving house	Lack of exercise
Too many jobs	Lack of daylight
Unrealistic goals	Diet/ weight / body image
Change	Guilt
Anger	Fear
Social media	
Resentment	
Comparing yourself	

You can use any of these words and more but remember the more specific you are and alert to changes in your mood the better prepared you can be.

SPACE IN THE BOOK FOR YOUR LIST OF TRIGGERS AND THOUGHTS.

OK so hopefully you have written down some things that affect you. To know and understand yourself you need to keep working on this everyday so be mindful about what makes you feel different ways; sad, angry, frustrated, negative, anxious etc. If you look at the emojis on a smart phone there are approx. 100 emotions and I for one am not aware of all the emotions in me and the difference between them, it is a learning curve and I am still learning!

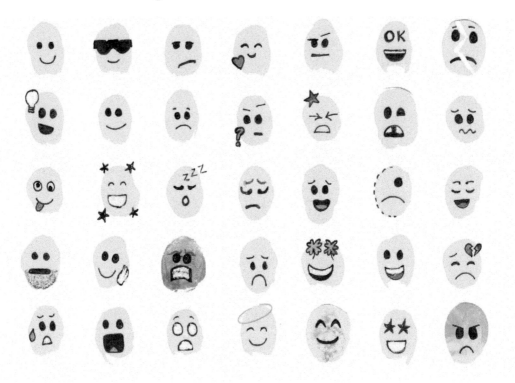

Looking at triggers for my moods a simple one for me is hunger, when I am hungry my mood changes and I get angry – or as we call it in our house Hangry. I am snappy at people and can't concentrate and I am irritable. I should know by now to eat regularly to keep my blood sugar at a sensible level but sometimes I don't and then I make poor decisions and cause stress for people around me. The solution is to eat little and often it is not rocket science, but we forget this basic thing.

Similarly, thirst is another basic thing we should avoid in order to help our bodies function and yet often I do not drink the advised 2 litres of water a day, even though it is free, and I have a tap with clean running water. I forget and get dehydrated ending with bad headaches and I wonder why!

Remember negativity breeds negativity and we need to keep our see-saw balanced. I would say remove all negative forces in your life where possible, but I appreciate that is difficult if they are a family member or friend. Instead minimise the amount of time you spend with them. These people drain our energy, they moan and are negative about everything and when we feel fragile, we don't have enough energy for people to drain our battery or for people known as "fun sponges or energy vampires". If you do have to spend time with these people then you need to feel on top of the world first, so you need to do twice as much good stuff to cope with them.

So, start small and think about your mood changes and triggers and start to identify them and once you know what they are, then take action to do something about it! I know there are more specific books on anxiety so it would be worth looking at those and other strategies to help you cope. But this is a good starting point and a step in the right direction.

I had a client that was suffering from anxiety and depression but liked to watch the news and keep up to date with current affairs. The problem was that most of the news on TV is bad news (I mean wars, famine, terrorism etc.) So, we suggested that news viewing was cut massively to help my client become more positive. The same could be said for social media, horror and disaster movies etc. Please be aware of what you are watching, reading, listening to and to whom you are talking and interacting with as all are potential triggers.

Take time to listen to your "self-talk" if it is negative and causing you anxiety and stress then you need to stop it. How? I hear you say, start with the basics and make a note of how many times you say can't in one day!

CONCLUSION:

KNOW YOUR TRIGGERS AND TRY TO MINIMISE THEM!

CHAPTER EIGHT
MIND GAMES

So why do we behave the way we do, well it's because we are animals and our brain reacts to circumstances in certain ways. Our brain is a complex organ, but for this explanation we can break it down into 3 main areas.

1. Reptilian stem   Ancient brain regulates breathing and blood flow
2. Limbic System   Emotional brain centre fight, flight, freeze
3. Cerebral Cortex   Thinking, logic, imagination

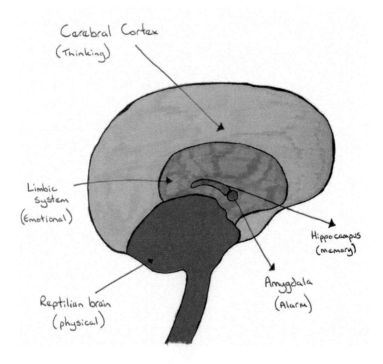

We are going to concentrate on the limbic system otherwise known as the emotional brain. In this system we have an area called the amygdala (shown as a red circle) this is our warning system so imagine that it flashes like an alarm when our brain thinks we are not safe.

When we were cavemen and a saber-toothed tiger was going to attack us, our amygdala would start flashing this is our basic response to a threat, it would then send messages to our adrenal glands to release adrenaline and we would either fight the tiger or run away. (Fight or Flight response) Our bodies also release the stress hormone cortisol as a little stress is good for us and keeps us on our toes. For example, not jumping off a cliff or picking up a poisonous snake. We no longer have saber-toothed tigers, but our limbic brain still thinks that there are many threats to us, setting off our amygdala and releasing adrenaline through our bodies.

Our amygdala (alarm) is also linked to the hippocampus which is like a memory bank of information. So, in an instant the alarm goes off the hippocampus checks our memory bank in nanoseconds to find a similar episode in our past to see how we should react. Unfortunately, the hippocampus is not 100% accurate and we are fooled into acting a certain way.

Let me give you an example;

My friend's son passed away at the age of 23 and this had a profound impact on her, basically she broke, she didn't leave the house, look after herself, engage with others the list goes on. A few years later she got the sad news that her mother was terminally ill, and she went into panic mode. I explained to her that her amygdala (alarm) had been set off by the news and it had checked with the hippocampus (memory) what happened last time someone died? My friend's brain was making her believe she would have another breakdown. However, after switching her logic brain back into play we looked at the differences of both deaths, ages, personal circumstances, health etc. and all were different this time. Don't get me wrong the death would be heart breaking but it would be different to losing a son.

Whilst our amygdala flashes it short circuits our brain and our logic thinking brain switches off. So when people say "I can't think straight" this is an actual thing. We are no longer in control of our thoughts and we get more and more anxious to the point of full panic attack. When your amygdala (alarm) is going off how do you switch your logic brain back on? It is really simple, – you need to breathe!

A simple breathing technique is to imagine a building brick;

Start at the bottom left corner and take a breath in until you get to the top left corner.

Now breath out from top left to top right

Now breath in from top right to bottom right

Now breath out from bottom right to bottom left

Kept using this technique until you have calmed down.

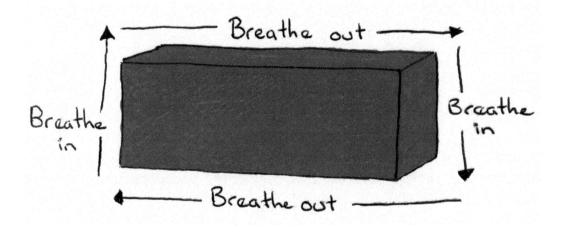

In our modern world we are surrounded by so much noise and chaos our brain perceives threats more and more often leading to high levels of cortisol and adrenaline running through our bodies. Our memory is full of episodes that have caused us fear and at any moment our internal alarm (amygdala) could start flashing from various triggers;

Loud noises, shouting, fire alarms, sirens, phones ringing, letters through the post, horns beeping, screaming, dogs barking, bangs, crashes, children crying, knocking at the door, heights, lifts, being asked a question, being centre of attention, escalators, crowds, people, bills, money, no food, shelter, safety, social media, news, radio, traffic, shops etc....

What happens to your body when your amygdala flashes?

Bascally, your body is flooded with adrenaline preparing you for a fight, flight, freeze response to a perceived threat, this is a basic human function and not your fault and this happens in a nanosecond.

You will experience some if not all, of the following symptoms;

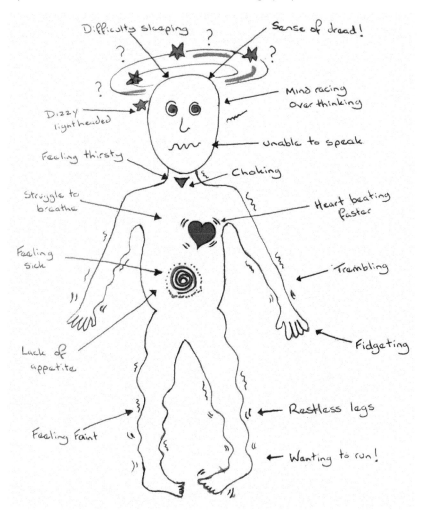

Difficulty sleeping ?
Sense of dread!
Mind racing over thinking
Dizzy lightheaded
Unable to speak
Feeling thirsty
Choking
Struggle to breathe
Heart beating faster
Feeling sick
Trembling
Lack of appetite
Fidgeting
Restless legs
Feeling Faint
Wanting to run!

Fight response is to attack, your emotional state is anger and you may insult, blame, attack and mistreat others.

Flight response is to hide, your emotional state is denial and you may avoid, omit or sabotage situations.

Freeze response is to comply, your emotion is to shut down and you may justify and rationalise the situation and give in.

What we really need to learn to do instead of the 3 things above is to face the fear – connect with it, understand it and get past it.

Next time you feel any of the symptoms, understand that it is temporary, the adrenalin in your body will subside. Use the breathing technique to switch on your logic brain and then analyse why your amygdala started flashing in the first place. Use your logic brain to override the memory bank as it is not 100% accurate and each experience you have in life will be different to the last.

We can retrain our brains to remain calm and take control back from our emotional brain, but it takes work and self-awareness of why your brain thinks things are a threat in the first place. We are not taught to recognise and understand our feelings, unfortunately in our culture in the UK we are taught to hide and ignore them.

I go on about this all of the time, saying we should teach our children self-awareness and how to deal with their emotions. My friend who worked in a school said to me that the school had started doing some work on this. They had got a mirror in the classroom and when the children came in, they were asked to look in the mirror and say how they feel.

At this point I nearly exploded. We can not look in a mirror and say how we feel, a smile on a face doesn't mean we are happy, tears on a face do not mean we are sad. Feelings are felt not seen! So, close your eyes, listen to your body, feel what is happening to your body and then you will start to understand how you feel.

"one of the best lessons
you can learn in life is
to master how to remain
calm" – unknown

CONCLUSION:

JUST BREATHE AND TAKE BACK CONTROL OF YOUR THOUGHTS!

Chapter Nine

Coping Strategies

After all the negative things we have thought about, there are also some positives in our life too. You are still here so whatever you have been through you have managed to keep going. That says something about your strength of character and your will to be here, you should be very proud of yourself, give yourself a moment to take pride in the fact you have not given up – YOU ARE A FIGHTER!. The fact you are reading this book means YOU want to change yourself and your life for the better and I believe YOU can do it. Try to look back and think about the ways that you have overcome difficulties in the past, would you do the same thing again or would you do something differently? Now we need to look at coping strategies!

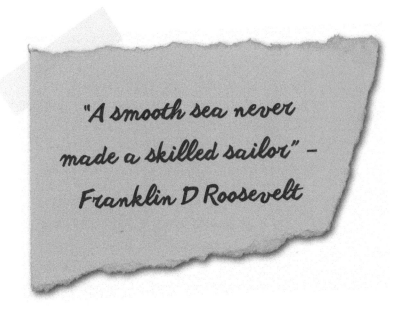

"A smooth sea never made a skilled sailor" – Franklin D Roosevelt

EXERCISE 8 — BOUNCING BACK

You may have hit a storm recently in your life or you may have been suffering in a stormy sea which seems like forever but there are ways to weather the storm and to become a skilled sailor to ride those massive waves. We are going to look back and make a note of how you picked yourself up in the past, it might not have been pretty and you might not want to do the same again but remember if you have done it once before, you can do it again.

It could have included; counselling, CBT, meditation, reading, writing, singing, dancing, baking, learning, crafting, self-help groups, church, sporting clubs, work, locking yourself away and crying for days, watching TV, walking, going to the gym, speaking to family and friends and much more including self-medicating (which I would avoid moving forward)

Think of one incident that made you feel crushed, sad or broken

Write down what you did to cope

1.

2.

3.

Be honest, some of my clients write, self-harm, drugs and drink and there is no shame in that, we are only human and do what we can at the time. Think about whether these things helped or could you have done something else? Preparation helps us to succeed so what we are trying to do here, is have a recipe for coping with bad things. If you didn't cope very well last time, write down what you will do next time should something bad happen.

What will I do to heal myself next time?

So next time I am crushed or broken I will…

1. Take time out and talk about how I feel

2. Ask for help (this is a massive issue for me but I know I need to do this)

3. Write things down

4. Dog walks, hiking, get out into nature and exercise

REMEMBER: HEALING = TIME + INTENTION + ACTION

What will you do to heal yourself next time you are crushed or broken?

1.

2.

3.

4.

I remember when I was really stressed some-one suggested that I joined the gym to help me cope with my stress. (This is one of my coping strategies) When I asked the guy at the gym should I do weights or cardio machines first his answer was, "it depends how angry and stressed you are," which I found a bit strange. But he said if I was stressed to get on the weights and get the aggression out of me, I have to say this approach truly worked for me. It might work for you too.

It is a bit of trial and error to begin with, but once you understand your moods and emotions and what you need to fix yourself or make yourself feel better, then you can take some control back and start to plan for the future.

EXERCISE 9 — MAGIC BOX

One of my clients who was recovering from alcohol misuse told me about a strategy that she used. She made a box (it can be out of anything you choose) and inside the box she made some cards which she wrote various activities on.

Clean the cooker, bake a cake, do some colouring, go for a walk etc.

When she felt low or needing a drink, she would get a card from the box and do that activity.

Give it a try, if it works great — if not then try something else.

EXERCISE 10 — MEDITATION TECHNIQUES

There is a huge amount of research that suggests mediation is great for anxiety, stress and depression. If you have classes locally give them a try.

If you prefer to try this yourself there are lots of aps you can download or checkout u-tube videos to help you get started.

My friend told me about an exercise that she practices daily. She got a diary which was based on Buddhism and mediation. In the diary you had to write what was stressing you that day. The diary had 2 columns, what is in my control & what is out of my control, once she started completing the diary, she realised that many things she stressed about were out of her control and she learnt to switch off and not stress about them.

Give it a try!

WHAT IS IN MY CONTROL	WHAT IS OUT OF MY CONTROL

EXERCISE 11 – DE CLUTTER

Sometimes our own environment is so stressful that we live in survival mode (amygdala flashing permanently) and it is exhausting. One of the things we can do in our logic brain is to simplify our lives and belongings.

There are many online checklists that you can access, or you can create your own. Think room by room. For example;

KITCHEN

1. Match plastic boxes and lids – discard any broken or lidless ones

2. Clean under the sink – discard old cloths, empty bottles, old cleaning products

3. Clean the oven

4. Clean the fridge – throw out old food and bits

5. Go through the cupboards – get rid of chipped cups, glasses and plates

6. Go through the cupboards – get rid of out of date, leaking food products

CONCLUSION: WORK ON YOUR COPING STRATEGIES!

Chapter Ten
Well-being

When we don't look after our mind, body and soul it becomes a vicious circle to get well again. We feel physically and mentally unwell and/or broken, which leads to us feeling less confident, anxious, down in the dumps and depressed. Prevention is the best medicine, so you need to listen to your mind, body and soul as it will tell you what you need to know.

The best way to analyse your feelings and understand them is to keep a diary or journal so you can see how you feel each day. Make a note of how much sleep you got, what you ate, where you went, who you saw and what you did. Believe me all of this will help you understand your moods and yourself better. Look back over your diary to see which days you had good days – who did you see, what did you do? It sounds so simple but once you identify what makes you feel better then; you need to do more of it.

If you didn't have any good days, then you need to start by looking at the five basics and check the following:

1. Eating healthily

2. Drinking water

3. Exercising

4. Sleeping (No caffeine allowed!)

5. Taking correct medication

If you are doing all of those things you need to look at who you saw and where you went and what the weather was like. You may also need to try something new. Remember if you keep doing the same thing you will get the same result. This is no good if it is not making you happy or content. It's very much trial and error and you will have to do a few different things before you know what suits you.

One thing I noticed from making a note of my moods in my diary was that I was a lot worse in the winter months. It turns out that I suffer from S.A.D otherwise known as Seasonal Affective Disorder. I now use light therapy to help me through the winter and darker days in summer, so just 30 minutes a day really helps as it gives me back the ability to feel emotions rather than feel nothing. If you feel you may be suffering from S.A.D. then discuss this with your GP or buy yourself a blue or white light – do some research first to see which the best light for you is.

EXERCISE 12 – DIARY/ JOURNAL

You will need a blank notebook or diary as you are going to record all of the following on a daily basis.

- » Weather
- » Sleep
- » Eating
- » Drinking
- » People you saw
- » Places you visited
- » News you received or watched
- » How you felt on a scale on 1 – 10 (use smiley faces if that's easier)

I would suggest writing a journal for a month, this is a commitment I know but the time you take to do this daily will really help you understand yourself and your moods and feelings better. Once you have written in it for a month then review your feelings and see if you can spot trends and triggers for your moods.

Over the page are areas that you need to start working on for your overall well-being;

Sleep pattern (When you sleep and how long) Try to get into a regular pattern set your alarm and get up. Try not to stay up all night and sleep all day.

Eating habits (What and when you are eating and how it affects your mood) Eating a healthy balanced diet is crucial for wellbeing and there are lots of books on healthy eating, recipes and ideas.

Exercise – do what suits your body and condition – sometimes lots of rest and sleep is crucial for your body to repair itself from illness so make sure you don't over-do it. Likewise, we need exercise to keep our bodies fit and healthy so there is a fine line between resting and doing nothing at all. If you don't know where to start or don't know what is good for you, speak to your GP or Practice Nurse. The BMC recommend 30 minutes of exercise 5 times per week.

Mental health – Keeping your mind healthy through exercise, learning, talking, activities that you like doing. (The secret recipe to happiness in chapter 11)

Loneliness – Feeling lonely and lost? There are lots of things going on in your area and lots of charities to help with social isolation. Speak to your GP, housing provider, Social Services, MIND and other charities or organisations to find out what is going on in your area. Check out your local library or go online for ideas. If you are at work speak to HR, your manager or colleagues.

Medication – Make sure you are taking prescribed medication only: it may be worth checking if you are taking multiple medications at the correct time of day/ night so have a review regularly with your chemist or GP.

Drinking/drug intake – Watch your alcohol intake and note this affects your wellbeing. Being numb is not a solution and exacerbates the problem. If you are taking illegal drugs or over using prescribed drugs seek help to stop this via your GP.

Relax – Take time out to recharge your batteries. Allow yourself to chill out and relax. Find something that suits you – different things work for different people.

Breathe – Yes we actually need to practice this one! Start by closing your eyes and take one large deep breath in so that your chest expands then slowly breathe out twice. Repeat until you feel calmer. Alternatively take a deep breath in and as you are breathing out visualise a word (that makes you calm) coming out of your mouth as you exhale. Practice, practice, practice.

Find something to do – Do what you like doing: a hobby or interest or volunteer in your local area, check at the library or go online to Do it.org to find organisations looking for volunteers in your area.

It's OK to say no – Remember sometimes it is good to say no, I am rubbish at this, so my top tip is to think before you say yes. Think whether saying yes is good for your health, remember your battery, if it is not full, then say no. We need to look after ourselves first and foremost. I really struggle with this as I feel guilty for saying no to people, but I realise now that my health must come first.

I saw a picture once that has stuck with me and helps me with my decision making of helping others as it reminds me to take care of myself first. It is similar to the battery analogy, but this works for me because I love tea. Imagine yourself as a teapot and you help others by filling up their cups, however, if your teapot is empty you cannot fill other's cups, you are empty and are no use to anyone else. Therefore, you need to take care of yourself first to ensure your pot is full!

Ask for help – Remember we are only human and need help sometimes, It's OK to ask. Make sure you ask the right people too!

" It all begins with you. If you do not care for yourself, you will not be strong enough to take on anything in life " – Leon Brown

After working with many introverts, I realise that they do not need people around them to energise themselves, they are fine on their own, so I appreciate that it is difficult to go out and meet new people. However just because your personality type doesn't need others to energise you that doesn't mean that your soul doesn't, maybe your soul does! Sometimes we need to push ourselves to do things that are good for us. (Mind, body and soul) Be Brave!

I know we all have off days and our body sometimes goes into self-preservation mode where it functions on a very basic level, to the point of just breathing is all we can manage and sometimes that is fine. Self-care includes chillaxing and doing nothing some days.

I have a client that came to see me, she was under the mental health team and they had referred her to my course. When I first met her, she could barely keep her eyes open, she looked broken and exhausted and I told her all she needed to do was rest or she would end up in hospital. There was no way her brain could function or even take in what I was saying but she was so conflicted as the mental health team had told her to get up and go out and keep her normal routine. I understand and say that to my clients all the time, but that is step 2, sometimes when we are truly broken, we just need to rest. I have been there and that is the first step to recovery it is hard to let others care for you and take over (because jobs are not done properly) but when you are so poorly and broken, learn to rest and let others help you. Think of the announcement on an aeroplane where they tell you to put on your oxygen mask first before helping others – it is lifesaving!

I took the lady home to her husband and she agreed that she would rest for the next week. She arrived the next week looking slightly better and continued with my workshop which proved really helpful for her.

The next step after resting and giving ourselves a little energy is to fight the urge to close our windows and curtains and hide away from the world forever. It really isn't good for our mind, body or souls. If you can start with one small step to help your wellbeing I would say **get up, get dressed, get out.** I don't care if it's pouring down with rain you must drag yourself out of your bubble. Your future self will thank you for this.

CONCLUSION: TAKE GOOD CARE OF YOURSELF FIRST!

CHAPTER ELEVEN

WHAT MAKES YOU HAPPY?

So enough of the heavy stuff, we have looked at burdens and loss, what makes you stressed, depressed and anxious, so keep working on this. You have some exercises (tools) to try and help you deal with these feelings but now it's time to find out what makes you feel better. It could be a long time since you last felt positive, happy or content but once upon a time you will have felt good. Or you may already know what makes you happy which is great. If you do know then the next step is to write down your secret recipe to happiness and make sure you do the things that make you feel better as often as you need to. Remember the see-saw. Keep that balance of good and bad in check.

If you don't know what makes you happy then let's try and find out. Please do not think that things or money make you happy, they do not. You make yourself happy, it starts from within, knowing yourself and feeling good from the inside. Sadly, some people could win the lottery and not be happy, because it would never be enough, they are not at peace with themselves and therefore will never be happy. Money gives you choices not happiness.

"If you want to live a happy life, tie it to a goal. Not to people or things." - Albert Einstein

The definition of happy is; *Feeling or showing pleasure or contentment*

If happy is a step too far let's just start with feeling content or having peace of mind and no suffering, stress, anger, sadness, loneliness etc. When I was broken my sister asked me the question, "What makes you happy"? I had absolutely no idea, I had spent all of my time putting others first, looking after others and thinking about others or work that I never had time to think about myself. So, at 39 I had to start to think about what made me happy. Our aim is for you to have your own recipe for happiness and to identify things that make you feel good.

Many of my clients really struggled with this one as it had been decades since they truly felt anything in their heart. They could go through the motions and exist, but never felt like they were living. I can totally understand this because when I was depressed, I celebrated birthdays, Christmas, girl's nights out, I joined in conversations at work and laughed and smiled and went through the motions, but I never FELT any of the joy. How could I when my heart was broken?

If you are not feeling it, I really do understand but it does and can come back if you work at it, just start small and work your way up.

EXERCISE 13 — SECRET RECIPE FOR HAPPINESS

So, let's start thinking about times when you felt calm and content, no anxiety, stress or depression. Try and answer the following to give you some ideas.

When was the last time you smiled and why?

When was the last time you laughed and why?

When was the last time you FELT calm and why?

When was the last time you FELT alive and why?

When was the last time you FELT content and why?

When was the last time you FELT proud and why?

Now think about what makes you FEEL content and write down the things you do (or should do) to make you feel better.

It took me a long time to make my own Recipe for Happiness so do not worry if you can't think of things straight away.

For example, I had a client who was suffering with a form of Bi-Polar, she had lost her way and herself and when I posed the question "What makes you happy?" she was unsure, after having a conversation and gleaning information from her she remembered she liked singing and going to church and crafty things. We discussed some goals and activities for her to try before her next appointment. She tried a knitting club but that didn't work, she tried a choir but that didn't work either and she tried going to church and she realised that was the thing for her. So sometimes we must try a few different things before we find what's right for us.

I did realise whilst writing this chapter that I need two secret recipes, some things to make me feel calm and less stressed and some things to make me feel happy.

Once you have an idea of the things that make you content start to write down your Secret recipe or formula for YOUR happiness. You can also write lists for helping you feel calm or energised or whatever it is you need.

If you need some help have a look at my lists, these took a few years to realise and no doubt will change as I grow as a person experiencing different things in my life.

MY TOP-SECRET RECIPE FOR FEELING CALM

1. Decaf tea (and biscuits)
2. Peace and quiet
3. Reading
4. Pilates
5. Sunshine
6. The sea and countryside
7. Walking my dog
8. Hot bubble baths
9. Watching films with snacks
10. Swimming

MY TOP-SECRET RECIPE FOR MY HAPPiNESS

1. spending quality time with my family
2. spending time with friends
3. Helping others
4. Hugs and kisses
5. Cleaning the house with music on full blast

6. singing & Dancing
7. Making dens
8. Playing trivial pursuits & quizzes
9. Learning new things
10. Travelling and seeing the world

THE BEST THINGS IN LIFE REALLY ARE FREE!

Some things I do every day and others once a week, once a month or once a year. But whatever your list is, make sure you know how often you need to do it to feel better.

I am very blessed and see my best friend every week and have lunch, talk about everything and anything and feel much better. It's about keeping in contact and nurturing relationships, so you have to make the effort too!

I meet the "Friday nighter's" every week, it's a bit like "Come Dine With Me", we go to each other's houses every Friday night and someone cooks, we eat, drink, moan about our husbands, children, jobs and put the world to rights, we laugh and feel much better for it. You could try and organise something similar remember; it's whatever suits you.

If you don't have family or friends and are feeling lonely then the best place to start is joining a club, church or doing some voluntary work where you can meet new people. Your local library, community centre or church will have details of things going on in your area or you can look things up online. You can also join on-line forums for any hobbies or interests you have.

If you feel you can't go alone speak to your GP about social prescribing or your local council about their strategy for social isolation, you may be able to get a support worker (like me) who can go with you. Or just be brave!

Please stop waiting to be happy. Telling yourself you WILL be happy when you lose weight, change jobs, move to a new house, find a new love, win the lottery. Sometimes it's about accepting what we do have, making the most of it as if it's our last day on this earth, because one day it will be. Happiness starts with you and you should feel it every day, not wait for it to happen, it starts with the little things, so start there and crack on.

"When I was 5 years old my mother always told me that happiness was the key to life. When I went to school they asked be what I wanted to be when I grew up. I wrote down "Happy" They told me I didn't understand the assignment, and I told them they didn't understand life. — John Lennon.

Do not overthink life and what your purpose is, let's start with – "Your purpose in life is to be happy" or alternatively your purpose in life is "Not to suffer". If you are content and have peace of mind and you make yourself happy then the world is your oyster and the rest will follow.

CONCLUSION: HAPPINESS IS NOT A DESTINATION — IT'S A WAY OF LIFE!

Chapter Twelve
Don't Compare!

To be happy and confident you must NEVER compare yourself to others, be it family, friends or celebrities. Unfortunately, the media is brain washing us to believe we are only happy if we are thin, with sparkly white teeth and live in a mansion in Beverley Hills, but this is not actually the case.

We are what we are. I am one of 3 girls all of whom are so different in height, build and personalities. I will never be a size 8 even when I was age 8 I don't think I was a size 8 and I am not going to waste my days on this earth trying to be – life is too short. I am a size 16 and feel comfortable in my own skin.

Once we accept ourselves and our reality then we have such power in our hands instead of being slaves to trying to be something we are not and didn't really want to be in the first place. All of this goes back to Chapter 3 – Self-awareness knowing who we are and Chapter 10 What makes us happy.

People spend a lifetime wishing for more money, clothes, cars, etc. always thinking the grass is greener on the other side – Well let me tell you something if you cared for YOUR grass yours would be green too!

So, make a start, start accepting life as it is and not like the pages in a glossy magazine. If you are not happy about your life, then DO something about it. As my dad used to say to me;

Knowing who you are, and your strengths and weaknesses will help you to stop comparing. For example; In the 16 personality preferences I am an ESTJ, I like order not chaos, I like lists and planning, I am good at helping others practically, I am an organiser and a doer, these are my strengths. My weaknesses are cooking, gardening, being spontaneous, being sympathetic, nursing people. My older sister on the other hand is a fantastic cook, gardener and is exceptionally patient and caring. We are all different, embrace your unique gifts.

I had always said to my mum that I would not care for her in her old age and that she must go into a nursing home. I don't care what others think of me because I know my strengths and weaknesses. My sister always said that she would take care of her. I think it's great that my sister could look after her, but I hold my hands up and admit it's not for me.

Learn who you are, (to do this you need to invest time in yourself) understand your strengths and work with them. Imagine if you invested all the time in yourself rather than others! Understand your weaknesses and work on them too, but don't let anyone make you feel guilty for who you are. Remember we are all different, embrace and love what makes you who you are, battle scars, heart breaks, physical attributes, mental issues and spirituality.

I absolutely love this quote, remember to LIVE YOUR LIFE not anyone else's.

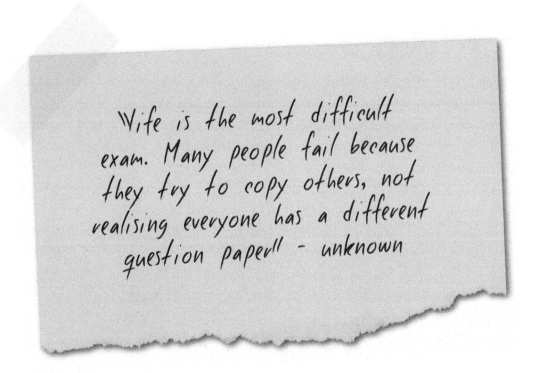

"Life is the most difficult exam. Many people fail because they try to copy others, not realising everyone has a different question paper" - unknown

Sometimes we feel a failure because we are compared to others in our upbringing and throughout our school and work life, as it is others who compare us to other people. Please remember no two humans are the same and all have different strengths. If you compare yourself with others – PLEASE STOP!

" Everybody is a genius. But if you judge a fish by its ability to climb a tree, it will live it's whole life believing that it is stupid." – Albert Einstein

I read an article recently that said, "Happiness is bad for the economy". It is so true because if we were all happy, we would not be insecure and feel the need to buy the latest cars, gadgets, houses and we wouldn't be trying to **Keep up with the Jones!** Advertising and media make us feel inadequate because it's big business – don't fall into their trap. In fact, stop getting the glossy magazines, stop watching the TV shows that make you feel inadequate, stop watching the news if it is adding to your anxiety and depression, stop using social media, it really isn't good for you! On the other hand, watch and use social media if it makes you feel good. I have lots of groups that I have joined on Facebook and would recommend; Word Porn, Just eat real food, The Minds Journal, Spirit Science, Positive Quotes there are loads of good sites offering some good advice (there are some you need to take with a pinch of salt too.)

I want you to feel happy in your own skin, be confident of who you are and what you want to achieve in life. So, let's keep this going, shall we?

"BE CONFIDENT. TOO MANY DAYS ARE WASTED COMPARING OURSELVES TO OTHERS AND WISHING TO BE SOMETHING WE AREN'T. EVERYBODY HAS THEIR OWN STRENGTHS AND WEAKNESSES, AND IT IS ONLY WHEN YOU ACCEPT EVERYTHING YOU ARE - AND AREN'T - THAT YOU WILL TRULY SUCCEED." - UNKNOWN

"Comparison is the thief of joy"
– Theodore Roosevelt

'We don't realise that we are actually perfect just the way we are. We are born perfect, but spend a lifetime trying to be something we are not, and then feel inadequate for failing. Your only purpose is to BE YOURSELF, otherwise you will deprive the universe of who you came here to be.'' – Anita Moorjani

CONCLUSION: DON'T COMPARE – BE YOU!!

Chapter Thirteen
Feel Thankful

If only you can see how amazing you are and be grateful for what you do have – not what you don't have. Sometimes we get so wrapped up in negative feelings it is hard for us to see the good stuff.

When I was depressed my sister bought me a book called "The Magic by Rhonda Byrne" and although I am not religious, one of the exercises in the book stuck with me. It is to write down every morning 10 things you are grateful for each day AND it has to be 10 different things. I thought there was no way I can do that but once you start it is amazing how much we take for granted.

So, my list went like this;

1. Waking up – I am alive yeahhh!

2. Daylight, sunshine, clouds

3. Opening my eyes and being able to see

4. Being able to hear

5. Being able to get out of bed – My health and my body working

6. Having a bed, quilt and pillows

7. Having a roof over my head

8. Going to the toilet – having a flushing toilet

9. Washing my face – turning on a tap and having clean water

10. Getting a shower –actually having a shower

Just think small, the list if broken down goes on and on. Think of nature: trees, the sky, the sun, the moon, birds, animals, hospitals, nurses, cars, radios, washing machines, paper, pens, staplers, schools, books etc. If only we take time to see how truly lucky we are, it changes our thoughts from negative to positive and really helps with our mind-set.

I do this exercise every morning when I wake up, only now I do it in my head. I also use this in my workshops with my clients and all feel the positive benefits of this. I also used to do this with my daughter. She was feeling very down and was questioning what was the point in living, as we die anyway. I told her to write down 10 things she was grateful for, then another and another, after one hour and 200 things later, she was bouncing on the trampoline saying I was magic. I am not magic – the power is in our own hands and minds!

Believe me this really works so now it's your turn!

EXERCISE 14 I AM GRATEFUL FOR

I know in the last chapter I said don't compare but sometimes we need to put things in perspective. So, I want you to imagine you are a child in a war-torn country. It is cold, the wind is freezing and howling around you, you hug yourself wearing a shredded nightdress covered in dust, your feet and hands are cut from flying glass and debris. Your home has been destroyed by bombs, as have your family, you are alone, you have no water, food, shelter, clothing or money, no doctors or nurses, electricity, or fire. You are lonely, scared, hungry, and exhausted. Now close your eyes and picture this scene for a few minutes.

Now I want you to look around and think what you have to feel grateful for. Write down as many things that you can think of and fill this page!

SPACE TO WRITE

I hope you have realised how blessed you are, it just highlights that we take so many things for granted. Please continue to do this every morning as it starts your day on a positive note and gives you a more positive outlook on life. Either write it down in a journal or diary or download an app. Some people use a stone or a pebble, trinket or piece of jewellery and every night before going to sleep they hold it in their hand and say one good thing that happened that day. Remember think small!

I have just downloaded an app called "gratitude" and every night at 9pm I write down 5 things I am grateful for that day. It certainly reminds you of what you have to be thankful for.

> "TODAY BE THANKFUL AND THINK HOW RICH YOU ARE. YOUR FAMILY IS PRICELESS, YOUR TIME IS GOLD AND YOUR HEALTH IS YOUR WEALTH." - UNKNOWN

CONCLUSION: BE THANKFUL FOR WHAT YOU HAVE!

Chapter Fourteen

Self—Esteem and Confidence

When I started working with people looking for employment, I noticed a similar thread running through all my conversations and it was that people lacked confidence. Because I was a qualified tutor I decided to write some workshops to help people with their confidence and what this highlighted was although I could train people to be more confident with employment matters like CV's, job searching, applications and interviews there was still a problem. Nearly all of my clients have self-esteem issues too.

So, what is the difference between confidence and self-esteem? Well very simply put confidence is how we are on the outside and our skill set. We can be a confident driver, cook, teacher, builder, public speaker etc. whilst self-esteem is how we feel about ourselves on the inside or what we see when we look in the mirror.

I have worked with many colleagues that have great confidence in their abilities at work, some lecturing to 100's of people and yet they hate themselves, their body image, they feel worthless, guilty, unworthy of happiness, to the point that they sabotage good relationships to make sure they fail, all because they don't like themselves.

It became apparent that my clients did not like themselves either, but I didn't see this as a problem just as a challenge as self-esteem can be worked on and we can change the way we feel about ourselves, to the point that we like and love ourselves deeply.

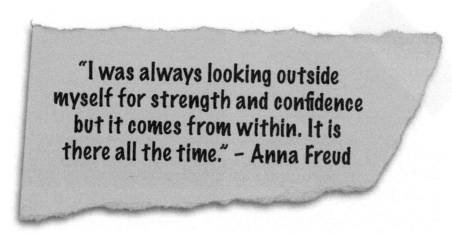

"I was always looking outside myself for strength and confidence but it comes from within. It is there all the time." – Anna Freud

Low self-esteem can be caused by many things, particularly our upbringing and relationships with others. If we are told that we are rubbish and will amount to nothing, then sadly after years of hearing it we sometimes believe it.

I have worked with many people and once they start following the actions to help build their self-esteem they don't look back. As with anything in life if we want to change something, we have to be willing to work at it; if you want to lose weight, get a better body, earn more money it takes work! Well, building self-esteem is the same. But please do not be put off, because if you have been doing the exercises in the book so far you have already made a start!

With regards to building your confidence, that too takes effort and I would recommend starting small doing little tasks and actions to help build your confidence. It is all about learning, being patient and not putting too much pressure on yourself. If you want to be more confident speaking to people, guess what? You actually have to speak to people. If you want to be a confident driver, you have to learn to drive. It is not rocket science. Be specific at what you want more confidence in and then start working on it or ask someone to help you achieve your goal.

You can do this by doing something little every day. I heard on a radio programme that a man who was scared of heights had challenged himself to climb over the O2 Arena in London. The psychologist on the programme said that he would actually be better off doing something little every day to help himself with his phobia. He compared it to learning to drive and having one driving lesson a year and hoping to be able to drive. We have to do something regularly to get good at it or make it a habit. He suggested that the man should climb a ladder everyday and go a little higher each time to help him rather than one-off large-scale tasks.

The other thing to build your confidence is to remind yourself that you are a good person and you will have done some great and good things in your life, only when we feel low, we tend to forget the good stuff. Reminding yourself daily of the good things will help build your confidence and self-esteem. You must also take time to be proud of these achievements. So, we are going to try and remember some of the good stuff you have done and write it down. Don't freak out remember we start with small stuff and work up!

EXERCISE 15 – WHAT MAKES YOU PLEASED WITH YOURSELF?

Remember your achievements; it could be anything from school, clubs, helping friends, family, strangers, lending someone something, going out of your way for someone, staying late at work, changing a shift with someone, sharing your time, lunch, home, car with someone, cooking and cleaning, giving birth, raising a family, buying something, providing for someone. This list is endless.

So now to begin, write down 10 things you are pleased with.

1.

2.

3.

4.

5.

6.

7.

8.

9.

10.

Great well done, take a moment to be really proud of yourself and give yourself a pat on the back. Oh, and you can smile when you do this!

Now how about your self-esteem? Well, if you have been doing the actions in the book so far then you have already made a start, keep up the good work you are doing great. Oh and if you have not started yet that's OK too but stop thinking about it, go back to chapter one and start doing!

10 ACTIONS TO BUILD SELF-ESTEEM

1. Know yourself   (Chapter 3)

2. Take responsibility for your actions   (Chapter 3)

3. Release your burdens and emotions   (Chapter 4)

4. Do things that make you happy   (Chapter 10)

5. Take care of you first   (Chapter 9)

6. Be kind and help others   (Chapter 9)

7. Ask for help   (Chapter 9)

8. Avoid negative people / places   (Chapter 14)

9. Set achievable goals   (Chapter 15)

10. Remain true to your beliefs

If you work on all 10 of these little by little on a daily basis you will start to feel better.

Remember what we have learned so far in this book and what we are working on to help us.

We have accepted what has happened to us

We have forgiven ourselves and others

We are aware of our triggers, resentment, anger, fear, stress and anxiety

We have put some coping strategies in place

We are doing the 5 basics – Eating healthily, drinking water, sleeping, exercising and taking meds/therapy

We have a secret recipe for Happiness, and we are continually working on this

CONCLUSION: CONFIDENCE AND SELF-ESTEEM IS A STATE OF MIND!

KEEP WORKING AT IT EVERY DAY

10 ACTIONS TO BUILD SELF-ESTEEM

1. Know yourself
2. Take responsibility for your actions
3. Release your burdens and emotions
4. Do things that make you happy
5. Take care of you first
6. Be kind and help others
7. Ask for help
8. Avoid negative people / places
9. Set achievable goals
10. Remain true to your beliefs

CUT THIS OUT & STICK IT SOMEWHERE TO REMIND
YOURSELF OF WHAT YOU NEED TO DO!

103

CHAPTER FIFTEEN
POSITIVE MENTAL ATTITUDE (PMA)

I have a positive attitude and always have, I have always felt grateful for my life and know that I have a great life, healthy children, a good job etc. but that doesn't stop me feeling low or nothing at all for that matter. I have clients that are clinically depressed and are essentially very positive people knowing that there are others much worse off than ourselves and yet we still feel down and depressed. This next chapter is to help us build our positive mental attitude to help us cope with stressful and difficult times in our lives.

Did you know that the Chinese symbol for crisis and opportunity are the same?

This is the symbol and it essentially means that in every crisis there is an opportunity. A bit like the saying "every cloud has a silver lining". Although difficult external factors affect our life we must be able to see the positive in each situation. For example, my dad dying was very sad and a terrible loss however it was also a blessing, because we  did not want to see the person we loved, a 15 stone man that had shrivelled to a 6 stone bag of bones suffer any more. I am not saying this is easy by any means but we must always seek the good in any time of crisis or difficulty.

You may have noticed by now that I like my lists, it's part of my OCD and a bit of an autistic trait I think, but never the less I am going to give you another 10 steps to help build a Positive Mental Attitude and you will notice that some of these are similar if not the same as building your self-esteem. That is because our confidence, self-esteem and positive mental attitude are all a state of mind!

> "Be careful of your thoughts, for thoughts become your words. Becareful of your words for words become your actions. Becareful of your actions for actions become your habits. Be careful of your habits for habits become your character. Becareful of your character for your character becomes your destiny." Chinese proverb author unknown

10 STEPS TO BUILD A POSITIVE MENTAL ATTITUDE

1. Know yourself and believe in yourself

   Knowing what makes you feel good and bad

2. Keep building your confidence and self-esteem

   Look at the actions in chapter 13

3. Where there is a will there's a way

   If you really want to do something you will find a way, that is what determines success, if not you will find an excuse.

4. Mix with positive people

     Avoid people and situations that are negative and drain you.
     Remember; move – you are not a tree!

5. Give things a go with a smile

     What is the worst that can happen?
     You only live once and more people regret the stuff
     they didn't do SO go do it – BE BRAVE!

6. WWW / EBI

     Always try to learn and do better in every area of your life.
     They teach this in schools which is great, look at
     What Went Well (WWW) and Even Better If (EBI)

7. Look at the bigger picture

     Before you judge a situation try to look into the future.
     For example, I have taken jobs that don't pay well
     but the training and career progression has been worth it.

8. Be kind to others

     It only takes a minute to thank and give praise to someone;
     a teacher, waitress, cleaner, shop keeper, family, friends etc.
     It is a win win situation, they feel better and you do too.

9. Crisis & Opportunity

     Remember to look for the good in every moment of crisis.
     In the recent bombings in Manchester I remember someone saying
     "Always look for the helpers" they are there and there is good in the world.

10. Set achievable goals

If we don't set goals our lives will amble on, setting goals
and ways of achieving them is great otherwise they remain
a wish that will never come true!

I love positive affirmations and quotes to remind me to think, feel and be positive. My house is full of signs, my latest one at the bottom of my stairs which I see every morning is.

THINK HAPPY, BE HAPPY!

It's great to have reminders to keep us on the right track so put pictures or words where you will see them on a daily basis just to give you a boost and the motivation to keep going.

"Positive thoughts are not enough. There have to be positive feelings and positive actions" – unknown

" Your self-doubt does not define who you are or what you are capable of" – unknown

"STOP being afraid of what could go wrong and think what could go right" – unknown

"You are a fantastic human being, start acting like it" – unknown

CONCLUSION: PMA GIVES US HOPE!

CHAPTER SIXTEEN
GOAL SETTING

As you will have noticed in chapters about confidence, self-esteem and Positive Mental Attitude there is always something about goal setting. The reason for this is if we want to change ourselves and our lives it is more likely to happen if we have a plan or a goal.

Now the thing is with goals they can be tricky little things because if we set goals that are not realistic, and we do not achieve them we feel like a failure. This really is not good for us if we are already feeling low, anxious and depressed. For example, I have a client that suffers with anxiety and over thinking, and she loves to write lists of jobs to do just like me. But her lists are ridiculous (her words) and go something like this.

Jobs to do today

1. Hang washing out

2. Take the dog out

3. Ring Doctors re appointment

4. Repaint the bedroom and hallway

Stress is the difference between expectation and reality

I hope this made you smile because we are all guilty of it. I do the same thing and then wonder why I am stressed. For some reason we decide to redecorate the whole house before Christmas, like Christmas isn't stressful enough! So, let's start again shall we? Ok so you might need a few plans, lists or goals but all must be achievable, it is no good saying you want to lose 2 stone in weight by Friday on a Monday morning and then feeling sad because you didn't achieve it!

I had a client with a seven bedroomed guest house that she no longer used as a guest house and it overwhelmed her as to where to start to clear the house. So, her goal wasn't to write a list of one million things she needed to do but to start with a simple goal of cleaning out one kitchen cupboard. And guess what she achieved that goal and went onto the next cupboard until the kitchen was done. The she went on to the hallway and is working her way through the house. This is building her confidence, self-esteem and positivity. So sometimes when we are feeling fragile and unwell our goals maybe just to get up, make the bed, open the curtains and get something to eat. THAT IS GREAT. START SMALL AND WORK UP!

The other thing we need to do with goal setting is to be specific, because if we are not, then we don't tend to achieve our goals. For example;

My goal is to lose weight

This is not specific enough, it's too vague and unlikely that I will take any action to achieve it. But if I say I am going to lose 2 stone in 6 months which equals approx. 1lb per week for 26 weeks and I am going to stop eating biscuits and chocolate then I am more likely to achieve my goal.

Goals need to be

1. Specific

2. Measureable

3. Achievable

4. Have a deadline

Our next exercise is to look at your life as a whole, to see where you are now and where you want to be and to set goals to achieve this.

EXERCISE 16 GOAL SETTING

You will need 2 different coloured pens for this.

Make a mark in each section of the circle to indicate where you feel that you are IN your life at the moment. 10 is feeling great and 1 is feeling rubbish. Remember this is how YOU feel, not anyone else, so you might not have a partner or romance in your life, and you might mark it as a 10 because you are happy with that. Then with a different coloured pen mark where you would like to be in life in that particular segment. You should end up with 2 marks in each segment.

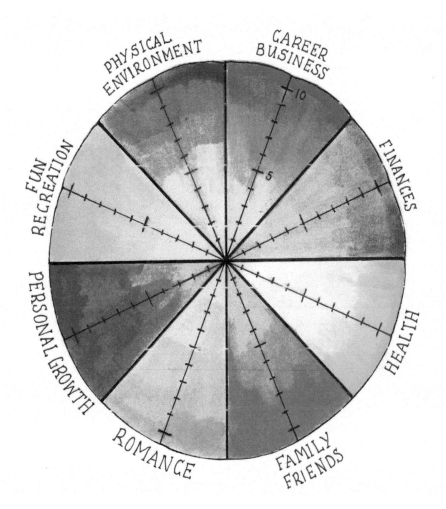

Now I want you to look at the difference between where you are and where you want to be in all segments and make a note of the difference around the outside of each segment.

For example;

Health might be 3 where you are now, and you want it to be 10 so there are 7 points of difference.

Once you have done the maths and worked out which has the highest difference choose the three largest differences. These are the areas we are going to use to goal set. We are not going to do all 8 at once as it is too much, and we will fail so a few at a time please.

Remember goals can be small and the deadlines can be very different. Some can be short term to do in the next day/ week. Some can be medium term, next 6-12months and some can be long term, 1-3 years.

Next, we need to write our goal, a deadline and steps to achieve it. Life takes us down different paths and sometimes we need to alter our deadlines so please don't be hard on yourself, just try to get back on track as soon as you can and remember you may need help and input from others to achieve your goal.

Look at my example which breaks the goal down into bite size tasks. Remember to be realistic. Why not get a picture of your goal and stick it somewhere you will see it every day? It could be to buy a car, going on holiday, new job, new house, peace of mind, stop smoking, stop drinking, lose weight, eat more fruit, drink more water. The choice is yours and if you have the will to do it you will always find a way!

GOAL 1	COMPUTER COURSE	DEADLINE
Step 1	Go to the library ask if they do courses	28 August
Step 2	Get number for the local college	30 August
Step 3	Ring college and get advice	30 August
Step 4	Check cost of courses	30 August
Step 5	Check bus times to get to college	5 September
Step 6	Enrol on course	8 September
Step 7	Start course	12 September

You may only need 3 steps to achieve your goal or you may need 20. Remember to keep researching and revisiting your goal especially if it is a long term one over 12 – 36 months as a lot can change in our lives over this time frame.

Be kind to yourself and keep working at it and if at first you don't succeed try, try again. Your future self will thank you for taking the time and effort to get yourself moving in the right direction.

Take pride in every step that you take to achieve your goal too. If you had not taken these steps, you would achieve nothing. We don't have to wait until the prize is in our hands, be grateful and proud of the little wins along the way!

Now it's your turn and remember to be specific.

GOAL		DEADLINE
Step 1		
Step 2		
Step 3		
Step 4		
Step 5		
Step 6		
Step 7		
Step 8		

"A DREAM written down with a date becomes a GOAL

A GOAL broken down into steps becomes a PLAN

A PLAN backed by Action becomes REALITY"

– Greg S Reid

CONCLUSION: SET GOALS AND SMASH THEM!

CHAPTER SEVENTEEN
THE WAY FORWARD

Now having read the book you have the tools to HELP YOURSELF, remember life is a marathon not a sprint so be kind to yourself and take time to heal. Imagine yourself as a machine that breaks every now and then, and you need tools to fix yourself. The exercises in this book are the tools and you can take them out of the toolbox whenever you need them. Remember prevention is the best medicine so try not to wait until you are broken. Give yourself a regular MOT, make time and invest time in yourself and your wellness – remember the teapot!

TOOLS IN YOUR TOOL BOX

Exercise 1 – Know Yourself

Exercise 2 – Visualise your burdens

Exercise 3 – Manipulate Burdens

Exercise 4 – Release the burdens

Exercise 5 – Mind Map

Exercise 6 – Visualise the See-saw

Exercise 7 – Know your Triggers

Exercise 8 –Bouncing Back

Exercise 9 – Magic Box

Exercise 10 – Meditation techniques

Exercise 11 – De clutter

Exercise 12 – Write a journal / diary

Exercise 13 – Secret Recipe for calm and happy

Exercise 14 – I am grateful for /good deed for the day

Exercise 15 – Achievements

Exercise 16 – Goal Setting

We also have the conclusions from each chapter too if you find that easier, just use those words to inspire you. Remember it's about you and what works for you! I hope this book has reminded you or helped you to know who you are, relit your spark and is a light in your darkness. Pick up this book whenever you feel the need and you will find peace of mind.

Better still get together with a few people that have the book and organise your own group to share your feelings, ideas and hopes and dreams with. You reap what you sow and believe me you could not put a price on the happiness I feel from helping others. I am feeling the best I ever have in my life and i am reaping the benefits of keeping my battery / teapot full.

CONCLUSIONS

SELF-AWARENESS IS THE KEY TO HAPPINESS!

IDENTIFY YOUR BURDENS AND FIND A WAY TO RELEASE THEM!

HEALING = TIME + INTENTION + ACTION

YOU ARE THE MASTER OF YOUR SEESAW (LIFE) — TRY TO KEEP IT BALANCED!

KNOW YOUR TRIGGERS AND TRY TO MINIMISE THEM!

TAKE GOOD CARE OF YOURSELF!

DON'T COMPARE

BE THANKFUL FOR WHAT YOU HAVE!

CONFIDENCE AND SELF-ESTEEM IS A STATE OF MIND!

PMA GIVES US HOPE!

SET GOALS AND SMASH THEM!

Thank you for buying and reading this book and working on your own happiness. I don't know where you are on your journey, whether you are in the pit of despair and need to climb out, you feel like you are going to fall in the pit, you are climbing the ladder out or you have climbed out and you are on the see-saw of life trying to remain balanced, but I know one thing and that is there is always hope.

The reason I called this book Keep Your Hopes and Dreams Alive, is because when I was depressed, I lost my spark, my identity and for a time my hope. But one day I found myself looking through some old photos and cards I keep in my purse and I found a gift card from my dad from Christmas 1999 with the words "Keep Your Hopes and Dreams Alive" that was a spark and it gave me hope and I mustered all the energy and will I had to lift myself out of the pit into the light again.

I got the words in my dad's handwriting tattooed on my foot and every morning after the shower getting dry, I look at the words and I feel them washing over me like a wave reminding me that my destiny is in my hands. I take action and invest time in myself to keep myself physically, mentally and spiritually well. I have learnt so much about myself since my breakdown and I have gathered the tools I need to keep my mind, body and soul in harmony. It is not easy, but it is doable.

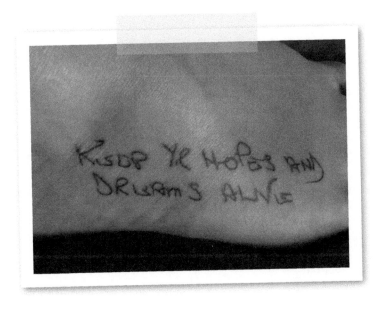

The reason for the dragonfly on the front cover has a few meanings to me also. I love dragonflies because they remind me of warm sunny weather and some of the amazing holidays that I have been fortunate to have. One of the holidays we had was in Turkey and every day when we went to our sunbeds a dragonfly would hover around us and sit on my sunbed or on our toes. Now I am not a religious person, but it seemed very strange that this dragonfly visited us every day and it just seemed special somehow. My logical brain can't comprehend spirituality and I struggle with things that cannot be explained but I like to think it might have been a sign from my dad that he was around watching over us.

The other part about dragonflies is what they symbolise which varies from nationality and culture but the one I found most relevant to me was the following taken from dragonfly site.com;

"The dragonfly, in almost every part of the world symbolizes change and change in the perspective of self-realization; and the kind of change that has its source in mental and emotional maturity and the understanding of the deeper meaning of life.

The traditional association of Dragonflies with water also gives rise to this meaning of this amazing insect. The Dragonfly's scurrying flight across water represents an act of going beyond what's on the surface and looking into the deeper implications and aspects of life."

This book symbolises change in you and your self-realisation to look deeper into yourself to find the answers.

«you've always had the power my dear you just had to learn it for yourself.» Glinda, wizard of oz

I HOPE this book has given you hope, inspired you and given you the motivation and will to make changes and take action, to heal yourself and make yourself well and to live a life with peace of mind and contentment. If there is only one thing you take from this book please let it be that you invest in yourself rather than others, you have so much potential, to live and create a life you have craved for so long. You CAN start afresh and get to know yourself, love yourself and you do have the right to be happy, that is your purpose in life. So now I will pass my message onto you as my dad did to me in the hope that it re-ignites the spark in you.

KEEP YOUR HOPES AND DREAMS ALIVE

On the 15 February 2018 my mum and best friend passed away. It is different this time as I am a different person. When my dad died, I felt relief that his eighteen-month battle with cancer was over but this time I was not ready to say goodbye. My logic brain knows I would not want her to suffer or linger on battling cancer or the effects of a massive stroke but selfishly I still want her here.

My heart is broken again, not the horrific explosion as it did the first time but the glue that was holding it together has gone. The physical pain is raw, and my heart feels like someone is holding it their hand and crushing it, there is a hole or a knot in my stomach which is causing me to gasp for breath. My body shakes uncontrollably convulsing and I break down in tears. This time I let them come, I will face this grief and despair head on, I will not bottle it up and carry this grief around with me. The pain is so hard to describe it's; exhausting, turmoil, brain fog and complete clarity of images at the same time, memories, memories, futures that will now not come to be. It is excruciating but I must let it all out, my courage is intact, and I know I will survive yet another storm.

I am calm now my head aches and my body feels broken, I let myself doze in and out of consciousness, nothing else matters but keeping myself well. I will heed my own teachings and ensure that I take care of myself first and foremost.

This time is different for another reason, my 12-year-old daughter has lost her best friend, partner in crime and nana. She is inconsolable, her pain makes me feel helpless and when she breaks down so do I. We cry together.

I know how to heal me, and I will do all in my power to ensure my children heal too. Already the lessons I have learned and shared with you are being put into practice. The basics of self-care, eating (even though I have no appetite) drinking water, getting rest, fresh air, dog walks and saying no because my battery is drained, and it is not good for me.

I make time to reflect and put things into perspective. I feel thankful and blessed that I had the best mum in the world. She was an amazing person, everyone loved her, she was a larger than life character and was known as "Mother" to many. Luckily, she was mine and I will be forever grateful for the 45 years that I spent with her and the time that my children had with her. She never said no to them spoiling them with her time and attention. She had no material wealth and her life was one of suffering, but she never closed her heart or turned her back to others. That is one thing she taught me and that was to always be kind. She saw the good in everyone and wherever she went she spread love and happiness. If I become half the women she was, then that to me is being successful.

Reading the diary that she left for us, it was clear how much she missed my dad, even though she never showed how heartbroken she was. I wander where I get it from? I like to think her spirit is now whole again and that she is back with her soul mate looking down on us.

As she got older, she got more forgetful, going through all the family names before she got to the right person, to be honest I have started doing the same! So, she got the nickname Dory from Finding Nemo, which was quite apt, because through all her suffering and difficulties she would always say, "Just keep swimming, just keep swimming".

Maybe that's the title for a second book?

UK Helplines

Samaritans	116 123
Childline	0800 1111
The Silver Line	0800 470 80 90
CALM	0800 58 58 58
MIND	0300 123 3393
Rethink Mental Illness	0300 5000 927
NSPCC (Adult advice)	0800 800 5000
Refuge (Domestic violence)	0808 2000 247
YoungMinds	0808 802 5544
Alcoholics Anonymous	0800 917 7650
National Gambling Helpline	0808 8020 133
Narcotics Anonymous	0300 999 1212
Cruse Bereavement Care	0808 808 1766
Rape Crisis	0808 802 9999
Victim Support	0808 168 9111